Swan Song

by
Len Baker
&
Rina Milsom

© Len Baker
© Rina Milsom

ISBN 1 870848 01 2

Other Books: 'Marlon' the Story of a Swan – Len Baker
'Of Swans and Other People' by Len Baker and Rina Milsom
'So You Want To Go Fishing?' by Len Baker and Rina Milsom

Design and Photography by Rina Milsom and Len Baker
(unless otherwise credited)

First published in Great Britain 1990 by 'Marlon Publications',
P.O. Box 3, Beccles, Suffolk NR34 0DF

© Marlon Publications 1990

Contents

Foreword

We are all, whether we care to admit it or not, benign destroyers of our Mother Earth. We use her resources to an alarming degree. We waste her bounty, with a carelessness that is beyond comprehension. We are all guilty. Some, through their work for a better environment, are striving against great odds to help heal the scars left by the careless. They deserve our gratitude and our respect.

Our planet is crying out for help. The cries can be heard from the animals and plants that are a part of this tiny blue jewel. There are those who hear the crying, and who soothe the dying, and there are those so preoccupied with materialistic gain, that their ears and eyes are tuned only to the sound of computerised profit.

This book is merely a diary of some experiences by we who have tried, possibly naively, to soothe the dying. At least we heard, and still hear, the crying.

We lived through the tears for twelve years. Through the deaths of some five thousand friends, feathered friends, with beaks and wings, but friends never the less. We, and they, suffered the procrastinations, deceit and lies, of a British Government and its underlings, totally dedicated to the political art of indifference.

We belong to a very small group of humans who know, through experience, that veterinary skills are important, and qualifications in medicine are obviously relevant, but who believe that spiritual compassion, when working with wild animals, is the most important attribute.

We have no formal qualifications whatsoever. All we have learned, was gleaned through living, and dying, with Swans. It was they who taught us how to mend wings and legs, when to treat sickness, but most important of all, when not to treat, but to give blessed relief, from pain and suffering. We had though, as a wonderful bonus, the help of a dear veterinary surgeon when really needed, but for the lengthy treatment regimes, we had only ourselves, to discover and perfect those treatments. There are no books available on the care and treatment of ailments suffered by a wild Swan. But then, there was no one working on Swans, every day, all day, anywhere in the world.

In a country where the "stiff upper lip" rules, emotion is not only frowned upon but regarded as a minor mental aberration. We are supposed to regard a wild animal or bird as a scientific subject. Swan-Cygnus Olor, certainly not Swan-Friend and fellow inhabitant of the planet. We can cuddle our Poodles (only if no one sees) but to see a Swan as another complete individual being, or worse, to love them for simply "being", immediately places you into a pigeon hole, labelled "crank". If emotions go hand in hand with being iconoclastic, then you really are in trouble and, if these ingredients of free thought are garnished with a touch of anthropomorphism, then watch out!

People working with wildlife in England must conform to the demands of the establishment to gain any credibility whatsoever. Work outside these boundaries and, however successful you may be in your chosen field, your chances of gaining recognition by those in authority are absolutely non existent. The fact that you have striven against all odds to establish "rights" for animals or birds, and in many ways have made great gains within your chosen field of animal welfare, will, paradoxically, go against you. For you have, by being successful, alienated the very people who are paid to care for Britain's wildlife. How dare you achieve success without the necessary formal qualifications?

If you are British, you are phlegmatic, if you are not phlegmatic, then you are obviously marching to the sound of a different drummer. If this is the case, then there is no room within the confines of the animal welfare establishment.

There, then, are two choices, either join the establishment and learn the art of procrastination, or work on the outside and do what you know is right for the animals or the environment. We chose the latter, and we, and the animals, are glad we did. In twelve years we attended but one meeting concerning Swans and lead poisoning. We lost time and money and the Swans gained nothing.

Another question that arises when you set out to work for wildlife, is a question that needs total honesty in its answer. Do you want to work for wildlife to satisfy your own needs, or for the wildlife itself? Does the satisfaction of your own ego come before humanitarianism? Do you need the thanks and praise of the people for saving the life of an animal or bird, or is it enough for you to be accepted by that animal or bird and be completely satisfied, and content, that that very acceptance is your reward?

As far as we are concerned, to be not only accepted, but also able, to live with Swans was more than a reward. It was a complete education and a wonderful, once in a lifetime, gift. For a period of our lifetime, we were surrounded by friends who were untouched by malice, hypocrisy or lies. It was only when we were forced to come into contact with our own kind, that we experienced these human frailties.

Apart from our precious supporters, we never received thanks, nor acceptance, from the British wildlife authorities. We were the biggest voluntary wild Swan hospital in the world, and from a population of some fifty eight million, only had four thousand regular supporters. It is therefore, as you can imagine, very difficult for us to believe in the myth that the British are a nation of animal lovers. True, we were invited to attend a garden party at Buckingham Palace, but could not spare the time to go as we were too busy rescuing Swans. Our refusal to attend this event led to our receiving many telephone calls from royalists accusing us of treachery and, at the least, insulting behaviour! In those days there were only four of us to cover the British Isles and Europe. At the end of our twelve year period of looking after the Swans of the British Isles, there were still only four of us, unpaid, full-time workers and four, unpaid, part-time workers.

In those, more than difficult twelve years, we had, without any financial grant of any kind, rescued some seven thousand five hundred Swans and had buried about three thousand. The two main causes of suffering and death for the Swans being Coarse fishing and overhead power cables, but the governing body ultimately responsible for the carnage of these beautiful birds must be the Government's wildlife "watchdog", the Nature Conservancy Council (NCC). Through their procrastination, over a period of ten years, their failure to reach a decision on the banning, sale and use, of fishermen's lead weights, resulted in the suffering and death of some forty thousand Swans. The NCC figures stated that four thousand Swans a year were dying through the effects of ingesting these weights. Their figures, not ours. Even to the time of the writing of this book, the NCC have only banned the sale, of "certain" sizes of lead weights. Swans are still dying of lead poisoning from fishermen's lead weights and of course, from the ingestion of shotgun cartridge lead. We will explain the effects of lead poisoning in waterfowl in greater detail, later, also the terrible suffering in-flicted upon wildlife by the ever growing "sport" of Coarse fishing.

Through the pages of this book we will attempt to show you the life of the Swan, and to take you upon a journey through twelve years of suffering, caused by the criminal neglect of a Government's indifference, and to expose the scandal brought about through the politicians refusal to interfere with a National participant sport. This sport is not only putting lots of revenue into the Chancellor's coffers, but also filling many spaces upon the voting forms with the magical "X" easily managed by the average Coarse fisherman. Do not upset the voter, old chap!

The following journey will, at times, be touched with sadness, but the happy and successful occasions, and there were many, will also be relived. Our only hope being that the future guardians of our planet will understand and recognise the beauty that is Swan, or Tree, Rock, or Toad. Magical moments, obviously beyond the comprehension of the cynic, will we hope, help plant a tiny seed of spiritual thought within the soul of the right thinking person, and that this seed could flourish into a new flower, of hope and faith. If the receptacle of this seed is a child, then the future of Mother Earth stands a greater chance. We owe this to the children, the inheritors.

When we started upon this unbelievable journey, we had no one to ask the many questions that so desperately needed answering. Perhaps this book will answer some of those questions and so enable the right people to continue to pressurise those in the higher echelons of bureaucracy, to spare one minute a day of their time, to ameliorate the remaining days that the creatures of feather, fur, leaves and scales, have left upon this overcrowded, tired, very tiny, planet.

Len Baker – France 1989

PART I

There once was a time
when waters were pure
and chemicals unknown.
Once – when the world
was young.

CHAPTER 1
The Early Years

In the late sixties I found the stress of trying to run a small business in England more than wearing. More of my time was spent as an unpaid government tax collector and bookkeeper than in actually manufacturing my product. The red tape that is so much a part of business life seemed to be strangling me. It was time for a decision. Taking Sheila and my two small children, Stephanie and Amanda, I ran away to Australia.

Aesthetically I found Australia stunning. It is indeed a wonderful country, the variety of its wildlife amazed me. I happen to love snakes and spiders. I think the great sharks are the epitome of evolutionary design. I rebelled against the gratuitous cruelty inflicted upon these magnificent creatures of the ocean.

Australia seemed to be, to my eyes, a country desperately seeking an identity. I feared that that beautiful country was tending to follow the worst of the American and English traits. I could not live in a world of fast food outlets and Bermuda shorts, introduced fox hunting and the English disease of trade unionism. I was appalled by the treatment inflicted upon the true Australian, the Aboriginal, I was also disgusted by the slaughter of that country's National symbol, the Kangaroo. The shooting of Brumbies (wild horses) from helicopters I considered barbaric, to say the least. These crimes being totally alien to my beliefs.

I was powerless to help. A "Pommie", armed with a briefcase, smart suit and cloak of naive ideology, was to say the least an incongruous spectacle. My protests then were unheard. My tail between my legs, I scurried back to England.

After rediscovering the country of my birth, the winding path of uncertainty found us back in Norfolk, where I had served for five years in the Royal Air Force. I would adopt Norfolk as our new home, but Norfolk never would or ever has, adopted me. I had remembered Norfolk as being one of the only places left in England where you could see the sky properly. Norfolk is a completely flat county and by chance, home of the largest population of Mute Swans (Cygnus Olor) in England. Probably the most commonly known area, within this county, being the Norfolk Broads (large areas of water), its rivers and its marshes. The Broads were formed by Man many years ago. Peat was dug for fuel and the diggings naturally flooded. There are five main rivers. The Bure, Yare, Waveney, Thurne and Ant. These areas of water and these rivers were to become my home, my classroom and my burden, for the next twelve years. I was to learn, through necessity, of all the secret places – the reed beds, the plants, the marshes and the dykes. These also, were home to the Swans.

I was to learn one of the most important lessons, the importance of Man to understand nature through all its complexities. But then to go further than simply understanding, to become "one" with nature. To look deeper into the relationship between Man and Bird, Man and Tree, Man and Water and Man himself. To actually feel a rock, rather than to touch it, to love and respect an animal or bird, rather than to own it. To never tire from learning, and to know you will never learn enough.

Until August 1977, I had never actually touched a Swan. I had seen them, of course, gliding upon the rivers and the broads but always regarded them as out of reach. To admire, to respect, but definitely not to touch. A strange bird, mystical but aloof, serene but awesome. Well aware of the myths surrounding them and fascinated by the making of these myths.

Upon arrival in Norfolk, I unceremoniously buried the briefcase, hung up the smart suit and set about seeking normality. As far away as possible from the world of cut and thrust, meetings and decisions, that are part and parcel of the environment that surrounds the would-be financial tycoon.

I would try and secure an "ordinary" job. Having always envied Ratty, from *Wind in the Willows*, I would try to find a job "simply messing about with boats". Sheila also secured a job and the children settled in their new school.

I soon settled into my new job at a boatyard in Horning, on the River Bure. I enjoyed the experience and was unaware, going about my work, that the lady Bure had started to weave her magical spell. I would spend my one hour's lunch break, watching the ever changing river and getting to know the animal inhabitants of that river. I watched the antics of the many Mallard, the Moorhens, the Coot, Great Crested Grebe, Canada and Greylag geese. The Heron, like a recently redundant undertaker, standing stooped on the bankside, surveying a likely victim, fascinated me also. I was totally captivated by one of my favourite creatures, "Ratty", the Water Vole. Lastly, the Swan family who, unknown by me at this time, were to become so much a part of my life.

I would arrive at the boatyard early and sit on the end of the quay watching the early summer mists lifting slowly above the reeds, break and allow a shaft of weak sunlight to dazzle the still surface of the early morning river.

Those who know and love the rivers will be familiar with the smell of a river waking into a new day, they will have heard, but not seen, the "plops" made by the riverbank creatures, dropping from their homes, deep in the riverbank, into the water, in search of food. Rivers, when devoid of people, are truly a magical place.

There was a place upon this riverbank, very close to the boatyard, where the branches of an old Willow tree just kissed the surface of the water. This place was to become my own personal sanctuary, my thinking place and my healing place.

It was at this place, during August of 1977, that I was to become involved with the Mute Swan. I had made a habit of taking an apple a day to work to feed the Vole, who lived below the old Willow. He would, nose just above the surface of the water, create a miniature bow wave, swimming toward my offered piece of apple. Holding his gift ahead of him, little back legs thrusting the water, he would scurry back to the bank. As I was watching the Vole I noticed something out of the corner of my eye. Floating downstream, just beneath a translucent layer of morning mist, was a white shape. It moved slightly. I thought at first it was a piece of polystyrene. What I had imagined to be an orange label, was, in fact, the Swan's beak. The black marks on the polystyrene were the Swans flippers. She was floating upside down. A pathetic, grubby piece of flotsam. She was completely wrapped in plastic, monofilament, fishing line and she was just out of reach from my side of the river. I panicked and shouted for help, but nobody heard.

Leaving this half dead bundle of feathers, looking tragically ridiculous, upside down, with its flippers slowly paddling empty air, I ran for help.

A boatyard friend fetched me a boathook but refused to accompany me on the rescue. He warned me that a Swan would break both of your arms, with but one stroke of its wings, and he disappeared back inside a boat, shaking his head and muttering. By the time I had covered the six hundred or so metres, back to the Swan, she had moved with the run of the tide and was lodged amongst the reeds in a small inlet on my side of the river, close to the old willow. I reached out with the boathook toward her and, in my attempts to connect with her body, splashed the water sending spray everywhere with the boathook in my crazy haste. I was sending her helpless body even further from the boathook by the waves I was creating.

I cannot, to this day, swim, a much desired prerequisite when one decides to rescue Swans! But neither could any member of our future Swan Rescue Service team. I have a deep fear, bordering on a phobia, regarding deep water. So it was with much trepidation I stepped gingerly into the shallows, holding my boathook at arm's length and moved toward the now very still Swan. The mud sucked me down to my knees. I was very frightened. In a last, desperate attempt, I lunged at the Swan. The tiny brass end of the boathook caught onto the fishing line and I dragged the helpless bundle toward me. Now I could not lift the body from the water, as I could not move my feet. The Swan, the boathook and myself, were it seemed, doomed to live there forever. I

struggled with the Swan, she did not move. After discarding the boathook I was able to lift the waterlogged body, I then had her securely in my arms. We both fell backwards onto the riverbank, my boots and boathook firmly stuck in the mud.

Nobody commented as I returned to the boatyard with my Swan, without my Wellington boots and quite saturated. The boatyard men smiled knowingly and went about their business. Loquaciousness not being practiced by the people of Norfolk. Wariness, and suspicion is, sadly, the order of the day.

Back upon the quay I started to try to remove this disgusting, cruel, invention – plastic fishing line. I eventually took seventy two metres of line, seven lead weights and a hook from this poor bird. The hook deeply embedded in the chest bone (sternum), needed the attention of a veterinary surgeon, or at least, an experienced animal welfare worker. I again asked the boatyard people for help. Was there a vet available? How do you contact an animal welfare group? A cleaning lady offered to phone a local inspector of one such group, but warned that she had never had success trying to contact him in the past. She was right. An answer machine advised her to contact someone, some sixty miles away, who was on standby. Not a lot of use to my Swan.

Meanwhile, back on the quay, the Swan had taken on a new lease of life. She was not now, however, the noble creature of grace and elegance, but a bedraggled, very wet and ungainly lady. She was now standing, but her neck was hanging to the ground, her beak dripping water onto the concrete quay. I had, in my panic, pulled many small feathers from her body, whilst unwrapping the fishing line. Some of these feathers were now floating, on the surface of the water, resembling tiny, white galleons.

I borrowed a pair of pliers from a mechanic and cut the cruel barb off the three quarter inch long fishing hook, after pushing the hook further through the bone of the sternum so the pliers would fit without cutting skin. The rusty shaft of the hook came away very easily. There was no blood from the chest but

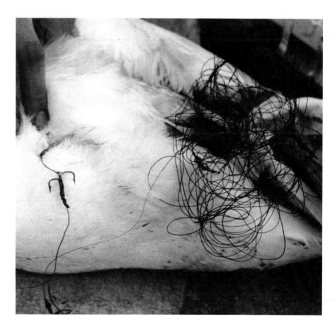

the fishing line had cut deeply into the legs. I had performed my first operation.

Now the Swan had rested, she became a white tornado. She hissed and flapped and staggered, like a drunken Ballerina in Wellington boots, towards the water. Making a loud splash as she tumbled down the three foot drop of the quay heading into the water. Without turning back she shot up the narrow dyke towards the main river. Her neck now strangely erect and slim. She disappeared with the speed of a white arrow.

She was the first. The mate of Marlon, a Swan that was to become a very great friend. I called her Pauline. The first Swan of some many thousands that would fall foul of this so called "sport" of Coarse (fresh water) fishing. When I questioned the men in the boatyard about such incidents, they told me that during the "season" this was an everyday occurrence. One man showed me the scars on the side of his hands received from fish hooks becoming embedded in them, whilst pulling hire boats onto their moorings by the use of mooring ropes, discarded hooks were embedded within the ropes. I was shown boat propellers completely wrapped in this nylon line, still carrying its lethal cargo of fish hooks and lead weights. Boatyard staff would cut these bundles of line from the propellors during boat servicing.

I could not believe, and still cannot believe, that in those days there was no one caring for the Swans upon our rivers and lakes on a full time basis and that this cruelty inflicted upon the Swans, although not necessarily premeditated cruelty, was unpunishable. It is paradoxical, to us within the Swan Rescue Service, that you can prosecute a lout for intentionally injuring wildlife by the use of, say, an air rifle, but you cannot prosecute the idiot within the ranks of the Coarse fishing fraternity for maiming or killing a Swan. In England, there are many laws, but hardly any justice!

For the next three years Sheila and I held onto our full time jobs and rescued Swans during lunch breaks and after work. During the fishing and holiday season, that is from April until October, we would average an eighteen hour day. We learnt a lot about Swans but the learning was difficult as there was no one to ask. Of course there existed the various trusts concerned with the breeding of waterfowl, but they then, and still do, tend to specialise in the breeding of "endangered" species and the release of these birds, into private collections, for a fee. Some of them destined never to feel and experience the magic of flight, as they were usually pinioned. They were to be gazed upon instead, by the uncaring eyes of the people of wealth and aristocracy. Wildfowl dealers still exist, unfortunately, in many countries of the world and will sell you a piece of spoiled perfection, for a few hundred pounds. You then place this piece of broken freedom on to your ornamental lake for your friends to ogle, whilst sipping their Pimms or Dom Perignon.

Wildfowl dealers, as far as we are concerned, are an anathema and the majority of them we have had,

through Swan reasons to contact, are merciless, cruel businessmen. Some of the smaller waterbirds are bred specifically to be released, full winged, to be shot from their sky, by the gun toting Hoorah Henries, that unfortunately breed like rabbits throughout the hills and dales of this green and pleasant land. But the word "shooting" has now become linked with the fashionable word "conservation". The green party member could be amongst these Hoorah Henries.

It is quite acceptable, it must be remembered, for the conservationist to enjoy Duck l'Orange! Somebody has to supply the duck. Conservation does not necessarily go hand in hand with animal welfare. The conservationists talk in numbers, population dynamics. We are concerned with individual suffering.

So we struggled on. We covered, in our very old Ford Cortina, the whole of the British Isles. The word soon got around that there were those fools in Norfolk that would actually go anywhere for a Swan in distress.

Finances were becoming very stretched. To buy petrol for the car we had to start selling bits and pieces of our home. We pawned Sheila's engagement ring and sold my record collection to raise some cash, and apart from the occasional "tip", from kind people, in appreciation of our travelling to an injured Swan, this was all we had. We were spending the whole of Sheila's wage, and two thirds of my own, on a bird we did not even own. But nobody had ever asked us to work for the Swans. It was, therefore, self inflicted purgatory. We were not unhappy with the situation. The Swans needed us then, and they still do.

There were now, with us, Swans rendered unreleasable through injury and they needed daily feeding. Wheat, the food of choice, is expensive. Pretty soon the number of Swans living with us in the garden of our farm labourer's cottage at Sparham, reached nearly two hundred.

We had become, through many television appearances and through the hundreds of newspaper articles published about our work, well known. But still, after over three years, no official help was offered, from any Governmental source.

We obviously made appeals to the many, supposed, larger animal and conservation charities, but to no avail. When seeking help from the World Wildlife Fund, as it was then called, we were told that Mute Swans were not an "endangered" species. At least the World Wildlife Fund had answered our appeal. Only three of our letters to the dozens of charities listed in the Charity Directories were acknowledged. We did, much to our surprise, receive from Her Majesty the Queen Mother, a cheque for £100.

So we carried on for another year and a half, on our own. During this time many Swans just did not respond to treatment. Way back in the seventies we were rescuing Swans, that seemed very lethargic, unable to eat and some weighing as little as 5 kilograms (a healthy female should weigh about 10 kilograms and a male up to 13 kilograms). These

Swans seemed to have a swollen lower neck, their eyes were ovaloid instead of round and their faeces was khaki coloured and very runny.

In 1979 I was asked by the local office of the Veterinary Investigation Centre, at the Ministry of Agriculture, Fisheries and Food, if I would take any dead Swan into them for Post Mortem examination. I complied. The results came back that the Swans had died of lead poisoning. Having too many Swans for the Ministry to handle, we started doing our own post mortem examinations. This was more than difficult. To cut a friend to pieces was spiritually abhorrent, but we had to find out how and why lead kills and find out we did.

The following may help you to understand more about this terrible toxin and perhaps, more importantly to make regular protests to your Government, pressurising them to implement a ban on all forms of lead used by fishermen and shooters. In these days of animal welfare awareness, it is totally incongruous to accept the use of a poisonous heavy metal whilst pursuing sport. The movement towards the use of lead free petrol, the removing of lead in paint and lead piping, is growing rapidly. Why then, should an innocent member of the animal kingdom remain last on the list of consideration?

As in common with all other birds, a Swan has no teeth. To grind his food to an acceptable digestive consistency he uses his gizzard. This is an extremely powerful muscle, located at the bottom of the oesophagus and proventriculus (glandular stomach) and positioned roughly between his legs. This gizzard muscle is so powerful that it can bend twenty two gauge steel and reduce flint stones to dust. When swallowed, food is transported, through the action of peristalsis, down the osophagus, through the proventriculus and hence to the gizzard. Before reaching the gizzard it is mixed with acids and enzymes within the proventriculus, to a predigestive consistency. Once in the gizzard it is further ground by the actions of the muscle and the use of grit. Grit is taken by the Swan to act as "teeth". Herein lies the problem. If, as in most cases here on the Norfolk Broads, the Swan has swallowed pieces of fishing line containing lead weights and these find their way into the gizzard, lead poisoning is inevitable. Also, whilst the Swan is taking grit from the river shallows and the edges of often fished gravel pits and lakes, he will obviously pick up some of the many thousand pieces of lead, that have lain dormant for hundreds of years. Lead does not lose toxicity with age. It is, therefore, an environmental time bomb, awaiting the unsuspecting waterbird. This lead lying around the water areas and estuaries of the British Isles, can also be from expelled cartridges, containing another lethal ingredient, Arsenic, usually used to harden shotgun cartridge lead. More about shooting later.

Because of their density lead weights, or shot, quickly drop into the gizzard. They are then already turned into lead salts by the juices in the proventriculus, ground down further by the automatic action of the gizzard and from there dispersed into the blood stream. The toxin attacks the central nervous system and slowly but surely, instigates paralysis of the muscular system. The incredibly long neck muscles are usually the first to be affected, giving the Swan a "kinked" neck appearance. The poison, however, has already permeated the internal organs and blood stream before this manifestation. If a Swan already shows a kinked neck, he is definitely beyond help. He continues to eat, however, but cannot digest his food. This food stuff builds up into a mass of rotting vegetation, bread, grain etc. inside his throat. The sphincters at the bottom of the oesophagus and from the proventriculus are now closed, owing to the cessation of muscle action through paralysis, also the sphincter from the gizzard to the gut proper. We have, upon post mortem, extracted up to two kilograms of rotting vegetation from within the oesophagus and proventriculus.

A cruel twist of fate designed the Swans intestinal system. Instead of a "straight through" system, as evolution has given us humans, the Swan has as part of the intestines, a blind ended gut. This is called a Caecum. The toxins now within the system are passed through to the Caecum, then at intervals unknown to science, are sent back to the intestinal tract and once again, via liver and kidneys, taken into the bloodstream. We know how often blood is changed within a human being. No one knows the time taken for a Swan to change his blood.

There are veterinary surgeons, and others, who to this day, treat lead poisoned Swans by intravenous injection of a chemical to chelate the lead within the bloodstream and, using calcium as a vehicle, to enable the Swan to excrete the poison. The determining factor used being the lead content analysed from whole blood samples. But what blood? Today's blood may have a different lead level, than tomorrow's or yesterday's. If we do not know how often a Swan changes its blood, how do we evaluate and measure the treatment? Ethylene-diamine-tetra-acetic acid (EDTA) is the chosen chelating agent. EDTA itself is a poison as it removes calcium, but is recommended internationally, in the treatment of lead poisoning, if given repeatedly for several days.

Remember that all the suffering and consequential treatments and therapy, bestowed upon the Swan, are the results of "sport".

It is true that some veterinary surgeons have attained reasonable success, in their treatments of Swans that are lead poisoned, but the success is usually derived from a decreased blood lead level. In the worst instances they have released treated Swans, back on to their rivers, only to be collected by us, in a few days time, dying from the same cause. Their blood lead level now showing an unsurprising increase. In the best cases, the blood lead level will be found tolerable, but the damage sustained by liver and kidney is irreparable. Through experience we have discovered that an acceptable threshold level of lead within blood or tissue, is unknown. This factor also depending, obviously, on the condition of the Swan prior to the ingestion of lead. In these days of mass development and exploitation of our water areas, by the recreation seekers, it is rare to see a healthy Swan. Their natural diets of aqua vegetation being ruined, long ago, by the selfish, uncaring managers of our environment.

Some veterinary surgeons and well intentioned amateurs also treat lead poisoned Swans before actually verifying whether the Swan indeed is suffering from lead poisoning. Internal injuries, Botulism and other diseases, can also be misinterpreted as lead poisoning, treatment for lead poisoning, therefore, adds to the suffering of the Swan. It is amazing, to us, that Swans are treated with dangerous chemicals, even before X-rays are taken, to determine the fact that the Swan has actually swallowed lead weights. To give a Swan chemical injections when there are lead weights actually present in the gizzard, is tantamount to giving a terminally sick cancer patient an Aspirin.

The recognised treatment for lead poisoned Swans, within the United Kingdom, was taken from a pamphlet issued many years ago, to doctors in New York, for the treatment of lead poisoned children, who had ingested small amounts of lead, by accidentally eating pieces of flaked paint, whilst growing up in the less desirable areas of that city. Flaking paint from doors, stairways and indeed old cribs, presenting a problem for the exploring infant.

This treatment regime and the chemicals used, were, it must be stressed, never designed or formulated, for the treatment of anything other than a human being. A bird's anatomy and metabolic structure, being obviously vastly different from that of a human, therefore rendering this treatment, at the least, very questionable.

The whole problem regarding lead poisoning, does not lie in the treatments used, but in the total banning of the use of lead.

It is an unfortunate fact that the more pedantic scientist, or veterinary surgeon, uses previously published, tried and tested treatment regimes, upon an animal or bird in their care. This, of course, in the terms of morality and convenience is perfectly acceptable. However, it would be better for that particular bird, had the treatments been tried, tested and proven, on that species.

In all our years of treating Swans, we have never seen a drug specifically designed for a Swan. Broad spectrum antibiotics, of course, are a different matter. We have used these, with great success, on cases of infection and disease. The respiratory disease of Aspergillosis, has been cured by us, by developing a special "tent unit", placing the Swan inside and, through an aperture in the side of the plastic tent, spraying the inside of the enclosure with a solution of Fungizone and water. This treatment produced a 100% success rate but only if Aspergillosis was diagnosed very early. Only experience, and the will to learn, will enable you to make the correct diagnosis.

We continued to rescue Swans and were amazed, constantly, at the amount of Swans that needed help in the British Isles. We worked long hours, with minimal financial income and not one offer of help from any recognised authority. The Swans suffered unbelievable injuries from fishing tackle, power cable collisions, oil slicks, road traffic accidents, lead poisoning and vandalism. Only a very small percentage of incoming Swans suffered natural diseases. For example, Aspergillosis, the respiratory disease, was usually exacerbated, through well intentioned people placing sick or injured Swans in their sheds, stables or barns, upon a bed of straw. The spores of this nasty fungus thriving in straw or damp vegetation. Mouldy bread being another supplier of these fungal spores.

We had a lot of learning to do, and at the same time were now supporting up to two hundred and fifty Swans, in our own small back garden. We dug ponds by hand, pumped them out and refilled them, and were getting very tired and disillusioned. After four years of this punishing schedule, Sheila's already dormant arthritis, now affecting both knees and wrists, was becoming very painful. To hand fill all the food bowls would take between four and five hours a day. In winter, before the bowls were filled, layers of up to one inch of ice had to be broken. Feeding had to be started well before we set off to our individual jobs. These were dark times, literally and spiritually. We would start the day in total darkness, and finish the day in total darkness.

Then springtime would come. The trees wore their new coats of green, the Swans contentedly preened in the gentle warmth of the early morning sunlight and slept by their makeshift ponds. Springtime would bring with it the promise of new life, new leaves and renewed optimism. This would prompt us to carry on, for the time being at least.

I advertised for help, and received many replies, but it seemed that the majority wanted to work on the

rivers with the people and boats. No one wanted to carry out the mundane tasks, of feeding and cleaning. Except one delightful young man, who was employed as a male nurse at a local hospital. He was quiet and unassuming, and seemed a thoroughly nice person. What happened to him gave me another insight into the Swan psyche. The Swans not only did not like him – but they attacked him. He was terrified, I was perplexed. Thinking that the red jacket he wore was in some way to blame for their aggression, I suggested we change jackets. He approached the Swans again, and again they attacked. The weaker Swans, in a panicked attempt to get away from him, pushed themselves into tight corners and refused to look his way. Our nice young man left us after two days. This weird attitude shown by the Swans, was to be repeated many times, in the future. The reason for their behaviour never being understood by us.

So the rescues kept coming, the phone rang all day, every day. The garden pens, during wet weather, became a quagmire. We would slip and slide and become caked in mud and still no offer of help. We made many more appeals and more television appearances, hoping that someone out there, in the real world, would help us to find a place for the Swans. They so desperately needed more space and better water.

It was, as you can imagine, very difficult for us to maintain any hope of ever finding them a place of their own. The local Naturalists Trust, the National Trust, the RSPB and local landowners were continuing to purchase many acres, of ideal Swan land, but never came to our aid. Oft-times our appeals were not acknowledged. This was to be expected from those bodies of establishment, comfortably ensconced within the environs of conservation. After all, Sheila and I had committed that most heinous of crimes, we had made "waves". The crime we had committed was this: When we knew who was responsible, for the suffering or death of a particular Swan, we said so, in no uncertain manner. When an angler left a Swan to die a lingering death, entangled in fishing line, we blamed the angler. When a Swan had its throat ripped with a fish hook, we blamed the angler. If a water authority had not acted promptly, to clear up an oil slick they themselves had caused, through their own well practised art of incompetence, and a Swan suffered, we blamed the water authority. If a power company, in Britain the Electricity Board, had been responsible for the suffering and death of a Swan, we blamed them. If a cretin with an air rifle maimed a Swan, we blamed him. So, if the Nature Conservancy Council ultimately destroyed thousands of Swans, by their criminal negligence, in failing to implement a lead ban for fishermen and shooters, we blamed them. We still do.

This is called "making waves". But this, let us not forget, is England. Fishing, shooting and pseudo conservation agencies are the establishment, and the establishment do not approve of the commoner making waves. You are, in your wave making, only rocking the boat of conformity. When you consider however, that the large conservation societies allow Coarse fishing on their, supposed, bird reserves, and the National Trust allow fox hunting on its premises, you should not be surprised that you receive no help from your pathetic, stillborn appeals. The rule is, "old chap", do not upset your membership. They after all pay your wages, and your mortgage, and put new curtains and carpets in your designer reception areas.

Within just about every country I have been lucky enough to visit, or to live in, there appears a moral dilemma that makes your living in that country a trifle uncomfortable. In my case, in England, it is the remnants of the class system and the malignant hypocrisy. In Australia, it was the transience of a, not yet established, culture. In America it is the disgusting waste of resources, food in particular, and the fashionable pursuit of self gratification. In the country I love most of all, France, it is the fact that the French are still suffering evolutionary misalignment and enjoy the disgusting, barbaric, neanderthal spectacle of the Bullfight. We will not mention Spain!

So for the animal lover, life will be pretty difficult anywhere in the world. But not as difficult as it is for the animals.

So we did not get help from the owners of the land and the keepers of the money. We would have to continue alone.

Or would we?

Centre of Norwich, Norfolk. The driver didn't even stop!

Victims of East Anglian power cables going home.

CHAPTER 2
Negligent Omission?

We were now into the 1980s, still rescuing, on call twenty four hours a day, every day. I had no choice but to give up my job in the boatyard, as I did not have enough time to concentrate on Swan problems. Sheila would remain at work to enable us to pay the necessary Swan bills. Wheat and veterinary surgeons fees were very expensive. Donations had increased, owing obviously to the continual publicity from the media. We now, at times, even had a full tank of petrol in the rescue car. It seemed a long time ago that I had to borrow three pounds, from a friend for petrol, to enable me to drive to an injured Swan, some seventy miles away. I still, however, had to find time to work on boat design contracts for new hull shapes for a company, in France. This work was carried out usually between midnight and four a.m. We needed this money to pay for our personal requirements and the rent for the cottage.

We were becoming well known now, by police forces throughout the country, and were getting calls from places as far afield as Scotland and the south of England, for Swans involved in road accidents or landing on motorways. It has always amazed us that the average policeman would not hesitate to grapple with a six foot, gun wielding villain but, when confronted by a startled stranded Swan, would turn into a simpering mess.

The look of relief upon the faces of the policemen when seeing the Swan car arrive was something to behold. Imagine then, their astonishment when a young lady got out of the Swan car, walked over to this white giant, bent down, lifted the Swan, tucked him under her arm and took him back to the car. Worse still to the machismo of the policeman, when the young lady weighed a mere eight stone! This experience did not win the young lady any prizes for tact or equality! In fact the reverse.

The fact that the Swan was on the main road was brought about by a common phenomenon, especially during wet weather. From a height of some one hundred or so feet a wet road, to a Swan, is a river. When there is a white line upon that road, to the Swan, it is his reflection. He lands, usually suffering leg injuries and a terrible shock to his pride!

The overstretched police force, cannot, at all times, stand by the Swan until you arrive. The Swan could, by the time you get to the scene, have already either wandered off or flown away. At the worst, he could have been hit by a car, or at best be holding up miles of motorway traffic. When you consider the implications of this, then you realise what a good idea it would be for a certain policeman within the local constabulary to be taught to deal with this potentially dangerous situation. To expect a tiny voluntary group of people to turn up on some far distant motorway, sometimes within minutes of the call, is to say the least a bit of a cheek. Imagine our feelings when failing to cover a distance of one hundred and twenty six miles, at an average speed of two hundred and forty five miles an hour, we were reprimanded for not being quicker! This happened on many occasions. We drew the line, however, when we received a call from a Gendarme in Lyon, France to remove fourteen Swans from the Peage!

Not all these happenings are tinged with sadness, however. There was the case of the Cygnet, not yet an experienced flyer, who landed in front of a huge truck on a main highway, the A11 from London to Norwich. The truck driver braked, jack knifed the truck and held the traffic up for some time. Leaping from his truck, he grabbed the startled Cygnet, sat him on the passenger seat and drove him the sixty odd miles back to his home, where he then called us to come and give the Cygnet a "once over". Apparently, the driver and his new mate, the Cygnet, had stopped at a roadside cafe and shared a pork pie.

We never had the heart to tell the driver that Swans are strict vegetarians! The little Cygnet was released after we had attended to the slight grazes on the soles of his flippers. We called him "Trucky".

I have mentioned my fear of water. In the early days we did not own a boat. We had in fact rescued some two thousand Swans before we could afford one. When needed, I could usually manage to borrow a row boat from either the holiday maker, aboard his hire cruiser, or from the boatyard that had called us.

Just before Great Yarmouth, where the sea accepts the waters of the Norfolk Broads, there is a vast, shallow area of water, known as Breydon. I have always intensely disliked the place. Apart from the channel across Breydon to accommodate large boats and holiday cruisers, the entire area, at low water, is thick, black mud. There are many legends and stories of dark happenings on Breydon. There, apparently, is a legion of Roman soldiers resting forever beneath the all enveloping mud. These legends have been built up over generations and are still heard amongst the mumblings of the riverside pub clientele, where old men with older dogs, in their chairs by the fire, regale the newcomer with tales of woe. They frightened the life out of me!

One afternoon we received a telephone call from a lady who lived close to Breydon, She had seen, or thought she had, some youths place a noose of electrical wire on a boat launching ramp where the Swans gathered to preen. When a Swan was in the centre of the noose, one of the youths pulled the wire. She was sure that the noose was now securely fast around the Swan's legs and, to make matters worse, these idiots threw the remaining length of wire high in the air. It had landed upon the back of another Swan. The Swans obviously panicked and became further entangled in the wire. The first Swan was now back in the water and virtually towing the second Swan, the wire caught, it seemed, under its wing.

I arrived at the scene within one hour but was unfortunately too late. The Swans had left and apparently were heading towards Breydon, the Swan at the rear had actually been seen to submerge. I ran along the bank as far as I could, but could not see the Swans. I then searched by car as long as the light allowed. I stopped, found a phone box and called home. Sheila had indeed received another call, the Swans had been seen on Breydon. There is a boatyard nearby where I knew I could borrow a boat. It was now dark. The man from the boatyard had gone home but finding an old wooden dinghy with one oar, I grabbed my torch, Swan hook and sliced bread, boarded the boat and set off towards Breydon.

It was hard work using only one oar and a heavy boat and I would paddle first to the left and then to the right, zig zagging up the centre of the boat channel, peering through the dark, hoping to see the two white shapes. From the little boat I could see the twinkling lights of a small village. I momentarily envied the very sensible people who were now probably settled down in their arm-chairs with hot drinks and an evening of television.

A fine drizzle had soaked through my cheap plastic over jacket and my left boot sole had a leak. I wiggled my toes and felt the cold water between them. There were now two to three inches of water, slopping about in the bottom of the boat. Slices of bread, spilt from the packet, were floating upon the water. As I was enjoying this sojourn upon the river, a terrible thought struck me. The lights on my car – I had left the headlights on to enable me to see whilst loading the dinghy. I could not remember turning them off. I did remember however, studying the packet of sliced white bread by the light of the car headlamps, checking to see whether the bread was mouldy. The fact that I had taken bread along, in an attempt to first feed, and then grab, two Swans on my own was, in itself, an act of committable insanity. It was not, it must be said, an act of sensibility to be here, on Breydon at night-time, with one, a leaking boat, stolen at that, and no life jacket. I tried to turn my little boat about to see whether or not my car headlights were visible. The tide had other ideas. I pressed on whistling a totally tuneless melody, that usually is a habit of the very, very frightened.

Then I saw them. They were struggling through mud. Through the dim yellow light of my dying torch, I could see that although black with mud, they were both alive. The Swan at the rear was almost on his side, one flipper threshing about, spraying mud like the propeller of a beached boat. It seemed as though the black plastic covered wire was, in fact, looped over one wing of this Swan and had been pulled tight by the terrified Swan, with the looped wire around its legs. I thrashed at the water with the oar and made very slow progress toward them. Sensing a predator, and obeying millions of years of evolutionary teaching, the front Swan speeded up, in an attempt to escape this apparition, with its one dim yellow eye and only one paddling flipper!

The Swans then became stranded in very thick mud and I gained a few feet. My trusty Swan hook, an old broom handle, with a stainless steel hook bent in the shape of a shepherd's crook, was about five foot long. I scrambled through the water and sliced bread, in the bottom of the boat, and stretched my arm with the boat hook, trying to reach the Swans. I failed by about three feet. Leaning over the bow of the boat, I could hear the sound of my own heart beat and the gentle pattering of rain upon the hood of my jacket.

Then I heard the voice.

"Oi!" It said. I listened. Then again came the shout. "Oi!"

I replied with what now seems, in retrospect, terribly correct English.

"Yes, did someone call?"

"Oi, you bloody fool, what's a matter, what you doin' owt there?" he asked.

"Trying to catch a Swan," I replied.

"What for?" he shouted.

"He's in trouble," I replied.

"So are you, old booty!"

I could now see the very welcoming, cabin top light of the little boatyard tug, the red and green lights of port and starboard. That dear old little tug boat.

"Stay where you are, old booty." My saviour's voice was that of the angel Gabriel, only with a Norfolk accent!

"I haven't much choice," I replied.

"'old you on," he shouted.

I did hold on. I was now pivoting, tummy down, across the bow of the boat. I had toppled forward, trying to lunge at the Swans, there was now, according to the laws of balance, more of me hanging out of the bow, and less of me in the boat. I must have resembled one of those little wooden birds you place on the rim of a glass of water. Having weights strategically placed, when pushed, these little birds would swing seemingly forever, beak toward the water and back again.

"Thanks for coming," I wheezed.

"You're right round the bloody bend!" he replied.

I rocked on.

"I'm gonna come up astern, 'old you on."

I held on, still gently rocking. The skipper of the tiny tug boat, with skill of many years and thousands of miles of river navigation, a craftsman if ever there was one, gently pushed the bow of his boat into the stern of mine. The bow of my boat dug deep into the mud and I joined the Swans, much to their surprise, to share in their mud bath.

I had them, or rather they had me!

I was floundering, crab like, upon the surface of the black mud and the skipper continued pushing my boat until the bow gently nudged me toward the Swans. He then left the wheelhouse, splashed through the water in the bottom of the dinghy and with his hand, the size of a shovel, grabbed my plastic jacket. The jacket ripped into two. He had a good hold of the left half. I had a secure hold of the black wire and my two Swans. They flapped, I flapped and the skipper swore. Then in a crazy flurry of arms, wings, legs and Swan hook, all were dumped into the bow of the dinghy. The skipper swore again.

"Completely round the bloody bend. From London are you?"

I held the Swans. The skipper ordered me to stay with them. I think I nodded. He then made a rope fast to the little wooden dinghy from the tug boat and we chugged back through the black water towards the boatyard. The now very low dinghy, two Swans, lots of mud and myself, being towed at two knots through the night. The skipper's voice transported by the wind, reached my dinghy.

"Bloody fool," he shouted.

"Thanks a lot," I replied weakly.

"Completely bloody mad," he replied.

Back at the boatyard I wrapped the Swans in a sheet and taped them together. I thanked the skipper and went to the car. The battery was flat. The skipper recruited someone leaving the pub, and he helped fetch a battery and jump started the car. Then the second angel appeared. The boatyard owner's daughter, with that most precious of all English treasures. Two steaming cups of tea.

"Thanks, Becky," said the skipper.

"You're bloody mad," said Becky, "completely bloody mad."

As the skipper was tying the now, half submerged, dinghy to the quay heading, Becky continued.

"Its no good using that boat, its got a bloody great hole in it!"

The front Swan did not regain the use of his legs for some days, the wire, tight around his thigh muscle had cut off circulation. In time he was released. The rear Swan suffered a severed nerve in her left wing and never flew again.

Back at the cottage in Sparham we continued to grow. The Swan Rescue Service was properly established and the Swans had their own bank account. We were now getting calls from all over the world for advice on the treatment of Swans. We were asked, by a large London publisher, if we would write a book on our experiences. Although I had religiously kept a day to day Swan diary, I could not find time to collate this information into a book. The publishers suggested employing a "ghost" writer. We agreed. Pamela Townsend's book *White Spirit, Fly Free* about our work with the Swans, was published by Sidgwick and Jackson in 1984.

Sheila at last gave up her job to run the small office at the cottage, to concentrate on mailing our quarterly Swan Rescue Service Newsletter. She had, over the previous years, rescued many Swans with me and on her own, and had nursed many to a more comfortable death. She still helped with the Swans in our makeshift surgery that was once our dining room. But the ever present osteo arthritis prevented her from physically helping with rescues upon the waterways and damp marshes.

We were to discover that the Nature Conservancy Council had been told of the lead poisoning problem, years ago. Indeed a paper written by Hunt and Simpson et al., had been published by Environmental Pollution, explaining Swan deaths and lead poisoning. Could the NCC really be guilty of negligence? Could they really allow this suffering to continue? Yes they could and, yes, they still do!

We wrote to everybody, who was anybody, pressing for a lead ban. We supplied pages of proof of post mortem reports from the Ministry of Agriculture after giving them hundreds of Swan carcasses. In fact we over burdened the good offices of the MAFF, so much so, that they could not in future take more than three or four Swans a week.

As we were, at this time, collecting over twice this amount, it was agreed that the Institute of Terrestrial Ecology, at Monks Wood, Huntingdonshire, take the remaining carcasses. They sent Mike French, who made regular visits to the cottage and took away many vans full of dead Swans. The carnage continued.

The Government would do nothing to upset the possibility of obtaining votes from the millions of anglers, so would not legislate against them. A lead ban would and indeed did, alienate this ever growing fraternity.

But what really could one expect from a Conservative Government whose hierarchy is made up by the type of typically English gentleman who peppered the English countryside with lead from their Holland and Holland, Purdey and the like, almost every weekend. We are still campaigning for the ban of lead shot used in these cartridges. We will never stop until we rid the earth of this lethal toxin.

We lived, and still live, in a different world from the peoples of power, the organisers, the meeting attenders. While they perform their rigid orders of protocol, the animals are suffering. Their suffering, though, received no audience and therefore no consideration, unless your protests went through the "proper channels", old boy! These meeting attenders are a special breed of people, they even have their own language. If you want to speak, you do so "through the chair" and you learn phrases like "point of order", which are the first words to come from your lips, on waking suddenly during the meeting.

After a few of these meetings a pile of papers is amassed and these are taken to someone else, checked and passed on to someone else again, are checked, ticked, added to and passed on again, ad infinitum. Then when many months have passed and another thousand Swans have died, or a forest has disappeared, or the rivers have been poisoned, the papers are put together, distributed in neat little bundles and given to the dark suited peoples of bureaucracy, taken to another meeting, glanced at, tea is taken, papers are returned, nods of approval are given, points of order are made and the meeting is wound up. The papers from the meeting are then taken to the copy machines and now resemble at least four elm trees, three ash trees or one and a half oak trees, of pure paper bulk. They then join the mountain of paper produced by other meetings and could, if the meetings were successful, end up within the bowels of the offices of the European Community. They are then, if fortune smiles upon the animals, made into laws. It is ironical, to say the least, that at times, these thousands of kilograms of paper could concern the terrifyingly rapid destruction of a forest.

This is the way it is, the scheme of things, the proper way. It is living in "the real world". It is democracy. Meanwhile the suffering continues and nobody helps, so you carry on. What choice do you have? You are committed, it is your fault, it is your problem. The Swan is, after all, only a bird!

He is also a warning. He is big, white and beautiful. When he suffers, so does the environment. He is easy to see, unlike thousands of the smaller creatures within our environment, whose suffering and death goes unnoticed. The microscopic creatures are also links in the chain of a secure and healthy environment. If we cannot take notice of the plight of the Swan, therefore, how can we hope to consider the importance of a blade of grass?

We never, in our wildest dreams, imagined we could save the Mute Swan from hurt and return him to a safe environment. We simply intended to make his journey, through this age of materialistic progress, just a little easier and more comfortable. In some ways, with some Swans, we achieved this.

We had been ready to stop our rescue service many times during these early dark years. But the Swans knew better and were to send us the people who would give us the strength to carry on. We now had two inflatable boats and engines, one bought through money raised by our supporters, the other a gift from Gorleston Marine, in Norfolk. We now had a better car, this time, a more modern Cortina Estate, enabling us to carry up to eight Swans, the boat on the roof rack and the outboard engine. A lady benefactor paid for a two way radio for the car which proved to be invaluable.

There were even rumours that the Government were considering the ban on the sale of lead fishing weights. One point concerning waterfowl and lead poisoning, never was discussed by the people within the animal welfare establishment. Literally thousands of Mallard, Pintail, Teal, Wigeon and wild Geese were dying, and had been dying for some time through the ingestion of shotgun lead. Many tonnes of this shot lies buried beneath the mud of the wildfowling areas of East Anglia and the other killing grounds of Britain. But people do not seem to get upset over a dead duck or goose. After all you can buy them from your butcher or the local supermarket. Ducks do not seem to evoke the same emotions that a dying Swan does. Tchaikovsky never did compose a work depicting a dying duck. A pas de deux for ducks contains no magic. You could hardly expect a myth concerning Leda and the gosling to stir any kind of wonder.

But the Swan, he is different, the "Royal" bird, the figure of mythology. The poor duck and goose suffers the same as the Swan. Lead poisoning is a terrible, unnecessary way to die, whatever the species. We were never able to save a lead poisoned duck or goose. By the time the symptoms were apparent, it was too late for that tiny body to respond to any treatment.

When you consider the size of this tiny, beautiful, British Isles and the vast amounts of people that inhabit it, it is no surprising fact that wildlife is being pushed out. We have taken most of their woodlands and their open spaces to build our concrete and steel necessities and pushed out the Fox, the Badger and the birds, to other areas soon to be populated with constantly breeding human beings.

Current economic practice and the introduction of more computerised technology have given priority to the pursuit of leisure activities. More and more recreational complexes are built and with the impending privatisation of water companies, more areas, or "playgrounds", will be made available. For the waterfowl this recipe is guaranteed to bring disaster. People are drawn to water. It is a magnet that attracts boats, surf boards, fishermen and jet bikes, skiers and canoeists, amongst the waterbirds who have nowhere else to go.

The Norfolk Broads and rivers have over two hundred miles of waterways. When I first discovered Norfolk, many years ago, there were places, so quiet that sometimes you never saw another human being. You could sit amongst the reeds and listen to the wind whispering music through the sedges, rippling the water and fluffing the feathers of the Swans and Geese. Feel the warmth of the summer sun upon your back whilst sitting quietly on a deserted river bank watching a beautiful, wooden yacht tacking its way up river.

Then someone invented the glass reinforced plastic cruiser. A floating caravan, easily mouldable and giving employment to unskilled labour, fresh from the labour exchange and the sugar beet fields. After very little tuition in the rudiments of laminating, these people went on to earn a better wage and a more secure future. The hire cruiser industry developed rapidly and devoid of competent management, these plastic abominations were soon to fill the once quiet waterways of Norfolk.

The "punter" could enjoy an affordable vacation and as a bonus be exalted to the heady position as "Captain" of his own destiny and five ton of plastic. Bedecked in nautical apparel, consisting of Aran sweater (with the sleeves rolled up), peaked cap with brass anchor, rope soled shoes and carrying nautical charts he could not read, proceeded to circumnavigate the island opposite the chip shop at Wroxham. Eddie Bush, living very close to Breydon Water, would be lulled to a contented sleep listening to the sounds carried across the water, on the breeze of the night, of the voices of these would-be Sir Francis Chichesters now very firmly stuck on the mud.

Nautical cries like, "Avast ye" and "ahoy there" and more frequently "for Christ's sake, HELP!"

They would only seem to come to Norfolk once, thank goodness, and obviously would enjoy the security of a council block holiday hotel in Majorca next year. Not for them the life of an old "sea dog".

A new animal entered the money making arena. The boat holiday broker. These aqua tycoons set up chintzy offices in the villages around the Norfolk Broads and using the mass coverage offered by television and tabloid papers, advertised holidays upon the Norfolk Broads. More boats were built and more holidaymakers came. Great plastic, waterborne snails, edging their way, stem to stern, up the rivers, during June, July, August and September. The once still, quiet rivers, now suffering the sound of a thousand radios tuned into mechanical disco music. The decks of the floating caravans decorated with various beer cans and half dressed, beer bellied

Careless boat users, sometimes resulting in injuries and death.

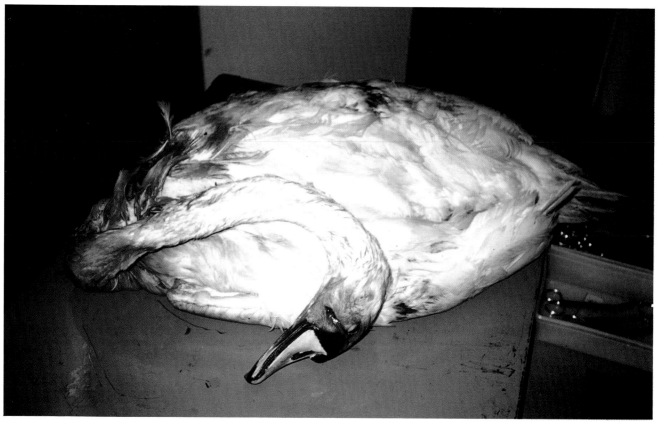

nautical experts shouting advice and abuse at other river users. Boats equipped with colour television sets and full inventory of human luxuries. Boats with propellers turning up silt and discarded fishing tackle, eroding banks and reed beds. (For which the poor old Coypu was blamed, and eradicated.)

Leisure totally beyond proper control and management. People who have never used a dinghy before are given a thirty odd foot cruiser, worth about sixty thousand pounds, with but one half hour's tuition by the hirer. The proper boatmen of old Norfolk, the Wherrymen etc., would turn in their graves, should they see the antics of these would-be Hornblowers.

But the holidaymakers bring money to Norfolk and who would refuse that? The hire boat companies, and in fact every boat owner, pay a toll, or tax, to the authority that controls, or is supposed to control, the rivers. What you get for your money is a uniformed inspector and his smart little launch. His job is to patrol the waterways and maintain law and order. But the golden rule seemed to us to be, that you mustn't upset the holidaymaker.

It must be said that there are some well behaved and very nice holidaymakers that come to the Norfolk Broads, for the right reasons. It is a shame that they can only enjoy their holiday, either in spring or very late autumn. It was usually, after all, the holidaymaker who called us to an injured Swan. We will be eternally grateful to them.

During late July and August, Swans gather in flocks to moult. An age old knowledge that there is safety in numbers, especially when you are flightless. The Swans of the Broads gather in areas like Surlingham, Rockland, Salhouse or Wroxham Broads. Fishing is allowed on these Broads. There is nowhere on the Broads that is now safe for waterfowl. It is an area of impending disasters, especially during the holiday period, from June until October.

A respite comes with the winter when the dykes start to freeze and the reeds are laden with tinkling ice. When the marsh grass crackles under foot and your breath freezes your mouth to your scarf. When the waterbirds are forced to scrounge for food, and the Heron looks for death, and the crows clear up the already dead.

When the early morning mists cover the marshes, and the overhead power cables become invisible to the Swan, you spend winter days clearing up their dead bodies and rescue the injured, from beneath the cables. Before removing the Swans bodies, we photograph them, take note of the power pole number and send this evidence to the branch office of the Electricity Board responsible for power cables in that particular area.

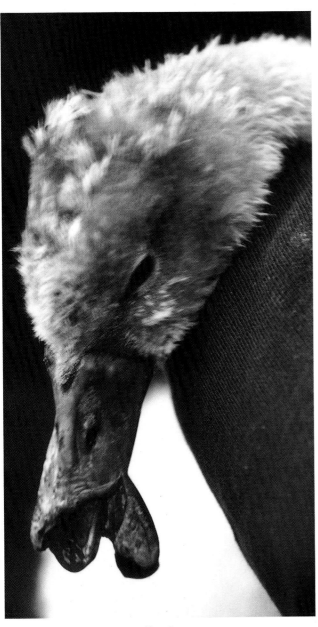

Propeller damage.

We also send the above information to both the Ministers of Power and Energy and the Minister of the Environment. It does no good whatever. But we persevere and will continue sending them. We maintain that in this age with massive advances in technology, to hang high voltage power lines from wooden poles, across the landscape of the British Isles, is to say the least, anachronistic. It is also an act of criminal cruelty.

We, and our supporters, have sent thousands of postcards depicting Swans killed by power cables to the relevant Government offices. Nothing has yet been done. Unfortunately, most of our Swans live in areas of marshland. The enlightened management of the Electricity Board tell us that they cannot bury cables beneath wet marshland. This, of course, is absolute nonsense. Electricity is imported from countries outside the British Isles. We have never seen a power cable stretched across the English Channel. It is, where all power cables should be, under the water! The only soft option carried out by our local and other Electricity Boards, is to fit silly little orange plastic spheres upon cables, in known Swan strike areas. These are about as much use as a chocolate teapot.

We have, many, many times, endeavoured to explain to the engineering managers and their bosses these obviously easy to understand facts.

A Swan has eyes on the side of his head, he cannot easily turn his head during flight. He simply is not made that way. He has, therefore, very limited forward vision. He can probably see the cables each side of his forward flight path, but sight immediately ahead is somewhat of a void. Consequently, the little orange plastic spheres, marking the cable, are in-

visible. Added to this is the phenomena known, of course, to many reasonable people, Fog!

Fog and mists usually manifest themselves at exactly Swan flying time. Early morning and late evening. Even if the Swan could see a power cable under normal conditions, on a brilliantly clear day, he could, like us, not see a cable shrouded in fog. If the orange bird flight deflectors fitted by the Electricity Boards were as large as ten foot in diameter, the Swan, nor we, would see them. Not in Fog.

These facts and the understanding of them, are totally beyond the comprehension of the officers of the various electricity boards. The only solution to the power cable problem, is to bury them in known Swan locations. Aesthetically too, the removal of poles, pylons and cables from the skies of the landscape of the British Isles, would be a blessing.

We have, very close to us, one power cable that stretches over the marsh, next to our Swan sanctuary. That cable has killed over three hundred and ninety Swans over a four year period. The cable supplies power to a riverside pumphouse, this pump maintaining water level over the marshes. In the days of civilisation this pump was a wind pump. So much for progress.

In Essex, at Mistley, there is probably the largest natural Swannery in England. Swans have lived here for many years. Above a road bridge, in Manningtree, there are, suspended from pylons and poles, a mass of high voltage cables. These are fitted directly across the Swans flightpath which they use for landing upon the waters of Mistley. Our Essex helpers, Bert and Joyce Green, are continually retrieving Swan bodies from the mud of this estuary, beneath the cables. When we telephoned the engineering officer of the Clacton on Sea electricity board, concerning the death and injury of these Swans, his reply was, "You're worried about your bloody Swans, what about the damage the things do to my cables!" He, in common with other engineering staff at the electricity boards, does not have the intelligence to realise, that if the cables were buried, there wouldn't be any Swan strikes. The burying of cables would also be of some comfort we believe, to patients dependent upon electrically powered Kidney Dialysis machines and the like. We wonder how much inconvenience was caused to the invalids of the British Isles, when cables were brought crashing down, during the 1987 hurricane!

The refusal to make life better for Swans and people, by burying power cables, is always that of cost effectiveness. Strange this from a company that proudly advertises the fact that they make over one million pounds per day – profit.

Heavy mist renders cables invisible.

Thousands of Swans each year are injured and killed by power cables.

"Flash over" burns caused by wing arcing.

CHAPTER 3
"Very Coarse Fishing"

Sheila and I were flagging under the weight of daily maintenance and rescues. I seemed to be living on sandwiches and eating them in the car, on my way to another Swan patient. A vacuum flask was the most important part of my equipment. At times I would not return home until the early hours of the morning. The summer months were still spent removing fish hooks, line, floats and lead weights, from entangled birds, and then releasing them back to their water, only to rescue them again and again. One Swan was dehooked and treated fourteen times before he was brought home for good, being too badly injured to remain on the river. I would fill plastic bags with fishing tackle and bring it back to the cottage, sort it out, list it and seal it into plastic envelopes for evaluation at a later date. Also keeping the fishing tackle was proof of the extent of the problem. The angling bodies, of course, still denied that their anglers were responsible. We were at that time, I am afraid, naive enough to believe that the more sensible and responsible angler would, wanting to clear their name, instigate educational programmes, aimed at the idiots amongst their ranks and establish some sort of guide rules. Apart from a little piece of paper, entitled "Anglers Code of Conduct" and the printing of "do's and dont's", on the back of a fishing licence, nothing was really forthcoming.

To make matters worse angling was, and is becoming, even more popular. Adding fuel to the flame was the fact that grubby, tabloid newspapers were offering large prizes for the biggest fish caught, of a certain species, in a certain area. Even more Coarse fishing magazines appeared on the newsagents shelves and videos were made to encourage this very primitive sport. It is still encouraged in our schools, in fact, in some it is on the curriculum.

During many years working with wildlife, it is of my opinion that the acts of cruelty, committed against animals, are usually perpetrated by people who have a deep fear of animals.

This will be well understood by a certain fisherman I met, on a rescue, one day in Norfolk. I was searching for Karl, an old Swan friend. It had been reported that one of his six week old Cygnets had been caught in fishing tackle and was in terrible trouble. The man who had called me from the Ferry Pub, on the river at Horning, had already exchanged words with the fisherman and had warned him that the Swan family were getting too close to his fishing tackle. The fisherman, in common with millions of other Coarse fishermen, refused to take his line and hook from the water when there were waterbirds about. (This carelessness and that of leaving an unattended and baited fishing line, has accounted for many deaths and injuries amongst waterbirds.)

Now it must be understood, Karl was a "warrior", a Swan of the old school. Nearly thirty pounds of white fury, though only when he had Karla and his Cygnets to care for (at other times he was a "pussy cat" but we never told anybody else this!) Karla was a very demure lady, in fact a tiny bit standoffish.

Arriving at their nesting site, on the bank of the Bure, opposite the Ferry pub, I could see that all Cygnets seemed to be laying around near and on their nest. Firstly though, I had to establish the whereabouts of Karl. He was, during the fledgling period of the Cygnets, the one to avoid, especially if you had to touch one of the Cygnets. Karl was nowhere to be seen. This was some comfort to me, owing to the fact that I was not looking forward to wearing a Swan and did not have with me any clean underclothing!

Proper schooling is urgently needed.

Unattended fishing rods cause many injuries to waterbirds.

Karla was some way from the nest, busily preening, but she had seen me. She had watched me arrive in the dinghy, borrowed from the pub, and had moved about six metres along the bank, away from the nest.

The fisherman had also seen me approach the nest and had now rowed over to my side of the river. He shouted as he approached, complaining that the Swans were a nuisance and would not stop taking his bread bait. He had paid good money for his holiday in Norfolk and was not going to allow filthy Swans to spoil his fishing.

He was the sort of person, I thought, that would have made a lovely stranger!

Karla was now getting suspicious, started to come back to her nest, her wings slightly raised and her neck straight up. I told the fisherman (using the Anglo Saxon language he could understand) to stay away and proceeded toward the Cygnets. Whilst indulging in the somewhat less than esoteric conversation with the fisherman, I momentarily lapsed in my vigilance.

The explosion came without warning. Clever old Karl had been watching from a tiny piece of water behind the reeds, some two metres to my rear. Water spray and white wings announced the arrival. I ran to the warm bundle of snoozing Cygnets but Karl outpaced me. Karla now had joined us. She, however, stopped short of the edge of the nest and Karl with his great black feet, planted firmly, but gently, amongst his offspring, protecting them with outstretched, two and a half metre wings. I grabbed frantically at the little Cygnet, clearly entangled in fishing tackle and stepped backwards from the nest. I was delighted, and very relieved, to be able to take the line off easily. I bundled the squeaking Cygnet back between Karl's legs, avoiding a feathered karate chop, aimed at my right temple.

I could hear the fisherman laughing. So apparently could Karla. With a speed that surprised me, Karla went waddling off towards the fisherman. For a second or so the angler froze, his face strangely contorted into a half smile. Then he ran and jumped into his dinghy, grabbing the oars, he paddled like a man possessed toward the safety of the other side of the river. Karla was now in the water and paddling after him, but faster than him. She overtook him and shot up onto the bank, his side of the river.

This, I hasten to add, was not an act of intelligence on Karla's behalf. It was simply that she was ploughing through the water at such a speed, that her own momentum carried her clear out of the water. In fact, she seemed very surprised.

The angler, however, did not know this!

I do not know how long the fisherman spent upon the river in his dinghy. The man at the pub told me that he was last seen heading towards Wroxham at an alarming speed. It is true that he did not return to his fishing tackle, that had caused this problem, until after dark that same evening!

One day after returning to the cottage at Sparham, from yet another rescue, Sheila told me she had received a telephone call from a man who said he would like to come over and talk with us about the Swans. They came that evening, he was Paul Scheller a graphic designer and his wife Sue, a teacher of pottery. There were involved with fundraising for Greenpeace and Friends of the Earth. When learning of the plight of the Swans, and us, they not only offered their help, as a rescue team, but proceeded to raise money for the Swans. They were more than welcome. We now had the help of this couple for the Norfolk Broads rescues, Jean and Kip Kirby for northern Norfolk and Bert and Joyce Green to cover Essex.

It was Paul and Sue that brought a very special present to the Swans. His name was Eddie Bush. Eddie was to prove the greatest friend the Swans, and us, ever had, and indeed still have. He is by profession an artist, a painter of rare talent. I have always been drawn to individuals and Eddie is certainly that. He is at home on the marshes and the riverbank, and knows and understands them. He is blessed with that strange quality, of silent communication, that animals understand but some humans find uncomfortable. Dogs, Cats, Hedgehogs, Swans and Trees recognise Eddie, not only as a friend, but as a brother. This, indeed, is a very rare gift. He can be stubborn, awkward, and at times slightly bombastic, but the greatest strength in times of stress.

On the occasions when we were all out on the marshes at late evening, searching for an injured Swan, when the darkness would start to envelop the landscape, the greatest sight you could imagine was the lone figure of Eddie, with Swan safely tucked under his arm, striding, Heronlike, back towards us.

It became commonplace to know that if Eddie went on a rescue, he would be successful. He would get the Swan. He preferred to work alone, and still does. This, however, is not as simple as it may seem. Consider this.

First, find the location, which could be anywhere in Britain, then the river, then the injured Swan. Try to catch the Swan, by hand from the riverbank. Fail. Unload a four man inflatable boat from the roof of the car. Unload then the outboard engine, fuel tank,

oars, life jacket, Swan hook, emergency surgical outfit, Swan wraps and catching bread and load into boat. Find, if you are lucky, a launching ramp. Launch the boat, fix the engine and set off. But which direction, up or down river? During the mundane, but very necessary preparation for the rescue, add to the anxiety you are feeling and the ever prevailing destructive action of stress. Stress, brought about by the fact that you know the Swan you are after could have a hook deeply embedded in his throat. The throat would be tearing by the pull of the fishing line, by the action of the Swan swimming fast away from hurt, the line, and possibly the float, in the water, trailing behind him. You see a group of Swans, but which one has the fishing line? If you have a bright day during your rescue and the sun on the water surface is dazzling, it is very difficult to see translucent plastic fishing line coming from the beak of a Swan. You then very slowly pilot your boat through the flock. Terrified now that your propellor does not come into contact with Coots, Moorhens, Ducks and other Swans.

You see your Swan, but now another traumatic split second decision has to be made. Do you use your Swan hook? If there is, and there usually was, a fish hook in the Swan's throat and you, with the best of intentions, use your hook on the Swan, will you cause even more damage to the Swan.

Remember that, as we have already mentioned, you and the Swan you are after are suffering because of a sport, perpetrated in the main, by little boys who have never grown up. It is not as though the fisherman needed his quarry to feed and maintain his family. This is sport. Blood sport.

Having located your Swan, because of the risk of using the hook to capture him, you decide to feed him with sliced bread, closer to the boat, hoping you can grab him. The other Swans and waterbirds surround your boat, tuned in to the sound of bread hitting water. Is your Swan amongst them? Swans are now shovelling the pieces of bread from the water, taking great beak fulls. You cannot, through this confusion, now see the Swan with the fishing line. Has he, in an attempt to take the bread, swallowed the line?

You notice the tell tale loop of line from the side of the Swans beak, you grab the Swan.

Now with the Swan in the boat, with trembling hands, you try gently to pull the line from down the Swan's throat. It does not give. You know, and only experience teaches you this, that there is a hook in the Swan's throat.

You now, on your own, with your Swan wrapped and sitting in the bow of the boat, head for the car. You put the Swan in your car and start to remove your boat from the water and load it back onto the car. Hardly ever are you helped during this process. A peculiar fact this. There are by this time dozens of people surrounding your car and making "coo, coo" sounds to the Swan, incongruously sitting in the back of your car. You struggle on alone. There seems to be no fisherman in your audience, just lots of people, that will agree with you on your criticism of anglers. They will probably buy their children little plastic "just like Dad uses", fishing kits from the many shops that litter the river sides of the holiday areas – the "tat palaces". It seems as though the vast majority of right thinking parents, in this country, consider that to go fishing is a part of the proper development of their offspring. "Boys will be boys you know!" The shops that sell this cruel rubbish, just do not, because of the governing need to make money, realise that a fish hook is a lethal weapon. They would probably, at least some of them, refuse to sell an air pistol to a child. We have lost more Swans through fish hooks in inexperienced hands, than we have through air gun pellets.

Where are you. Law makers?

The Swan, now in the surgery, is X-rayed, the hook is indeed deep into the throat. You arrange an operation at your veterinary surgeons, and he cuts the Swan's throat, to remove the hook. If the Swan is lucky, or if you are lucky enough to have an experienced veterinary surgeon, as was our dear Mr Barnes from East Dereham, a rare vet that would actually work on a Swan, then you take the Swan home stitched and bloody, to spend a couple of weeks in care before being released. If your Swan is one of a pair, and they have Cygnets, then the person that caused this injury has also committed another crime. He has, by his carelessness, separated, and through separation possibly destroyed, an entire Swan family.

After bringing the Swan home, Eddie would soon be on his way to another rescue, still on his own.

Multiply these experiences by about another two hundred and fifty and you have a rough, but only rough, idea of Eddie's summertime.

In the misty dusk of a late summer's evening, if by chance whilst holidaying on the Norfolk Broads, you caught a very quick glimpse of what you thought was a giant Turkish, grey Turtle, the long legged type, it was a good chance that you had seen Eddie, boat on his back, wending his lonely way up an isolated riverbank. Probably, soon on his way to another Swan. Alone to you perhaps, but with an unseen army of some four thousand dead Swans by his side.

That was then, and still is, Eddie Bush.

Eddie, Swan, and Rina on the way home.

The following pages show just a few of the Swans to suffer through Britain's biggest participant sport . . .

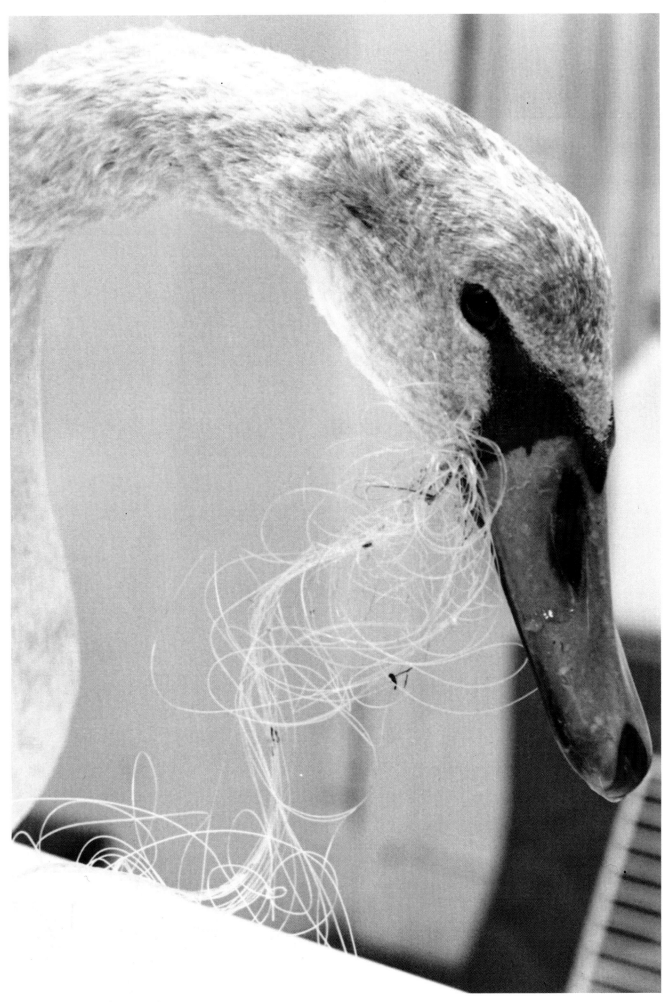

How accidents happen. Fishing amidst waterbirds, oblivious of the danger that is imminent.

Potter Heigham, Norfolk Broads.

Typical coarse fishing areas, Rollesby Broad, Norfolk, is very popular with experienced anglers and children owing to easy access. Every Swan that lands here and stays awhile, dies of either hookings or lead poisoning.

The photographs do little to promote a better image for the coarse fisherman.

During one and a half hours spent clearing the filth from the area above, we collected three carrier bags of tackle, lead weights and hooks.

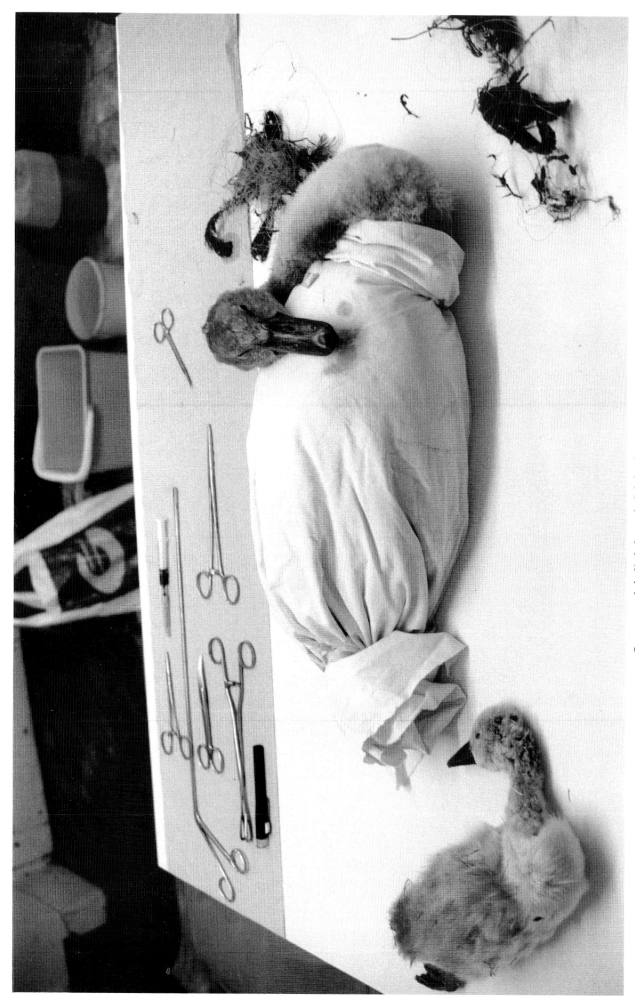

Cygnet on left died through fish hook ripping its throat.
Cygnet right was too ill to go through operation to remove three hooks from throat and gizzard. Put to sleep.

One season's coarse fishing. Every piece taken off Swans.

Our own outboard engine, after rescuing a Swan that had been hooked. Note the fishing line wrapped around propeller.

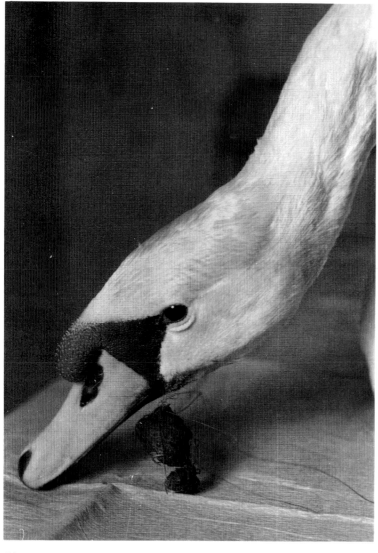

Left. Showing wad of vegetation from gizzard with hook in throat and line attached. Within the gizzard contents are three pieces of split shot.

Wroxham Broad. Hook in throat, line from beak. One of approximately 500 Swans rescued per year by us alone suffering fishing tackle injuries.

Tongue tied down, unable to eat. Starvation would have followed. River Wensum, Riverside, Norwich.

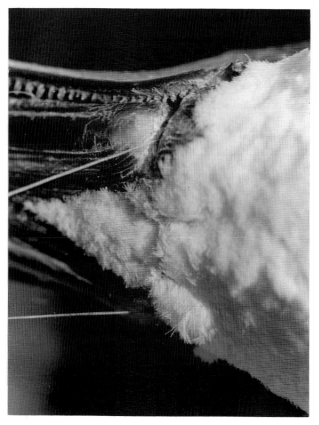

Line holding tongue down and thence down throat. Oulton Broad, Suffolk.

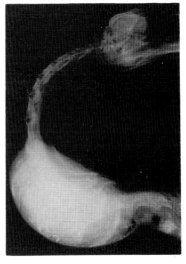

The fish hook as seen in the X-ray photograph (right), ripped the Swan's throat open. The Swan continued to eat and take grit. The food, and grit, was forced through the ripped throat into the neck, this year old Swan died an agonising death from starvation.

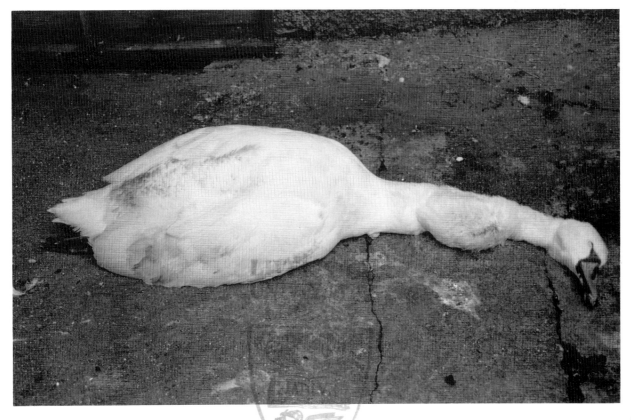

49

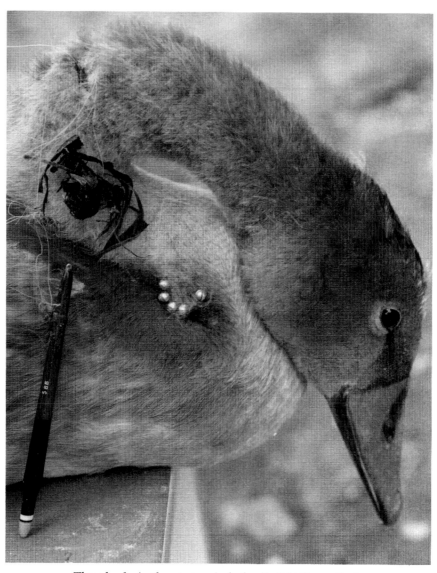

Three hooks in throat, two in body. Enfield Town Park.

Hook in throat, Wroxham, Norfolk.

50

Hook in throat, line hanging. Barnstaple, Devon.

Wells, Norfolk. Cygnet on left, hook in throat, line and piece of wood hanging.

Cheshunt, Herts. Death finally released this cob.
Large hook embedded in throat and line from beak (can be seen in water) 1988.

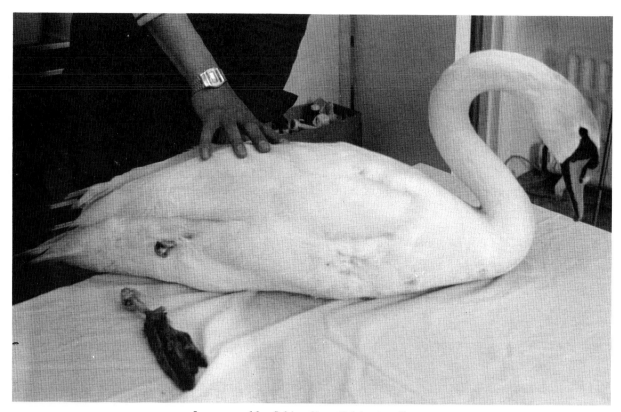

Leg severed by fishing line. Colchester, Essex.

It is obviously not only Swans that suffer.
We could not catch the Egyptian goose above. Her leg was almost severed by line.

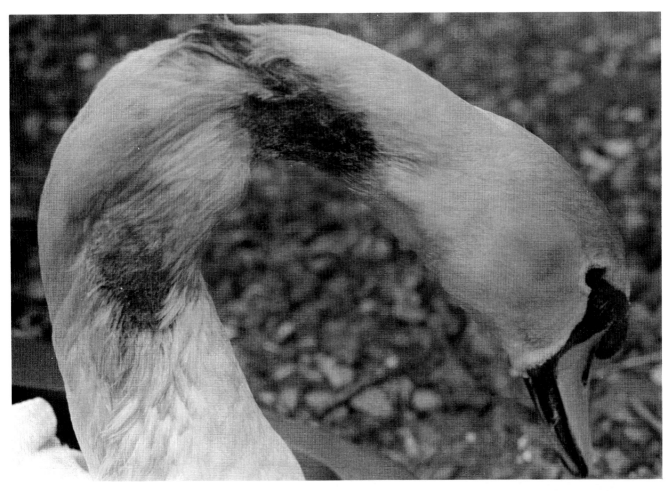

After surgery for removal of 2 hooks in throat. Line was caught round lower bill. Wellingborough, Northants.

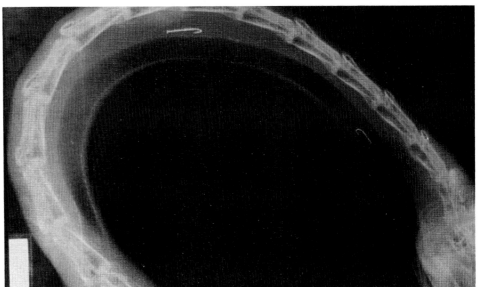

X-ray of hooks.

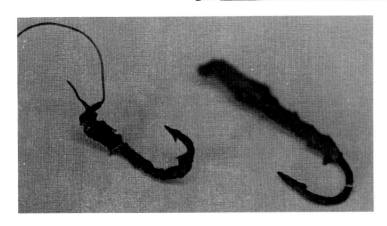

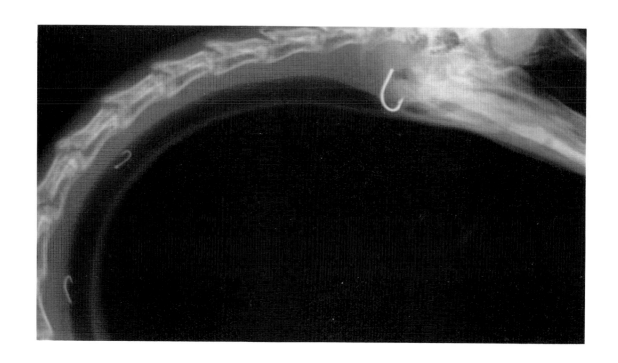

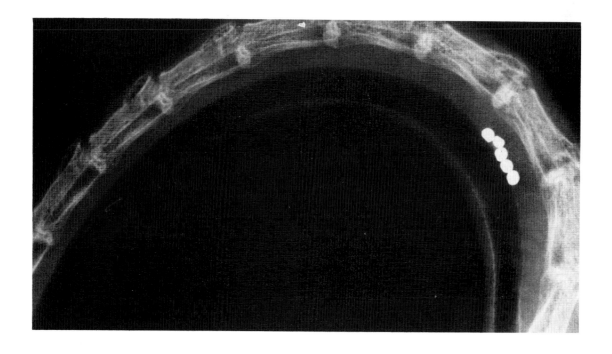

Typical X-rays.

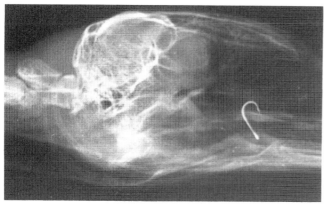
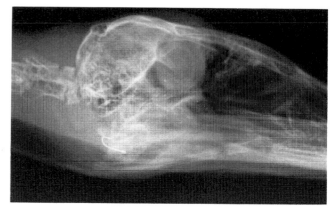

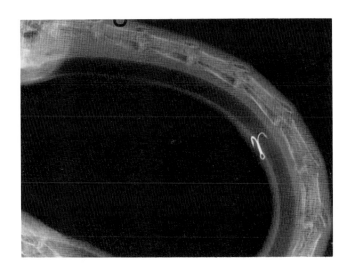
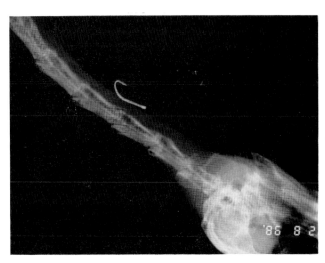
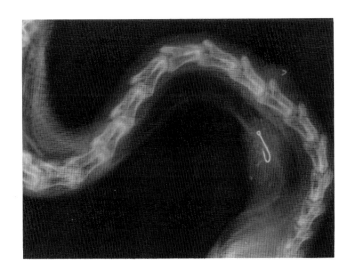
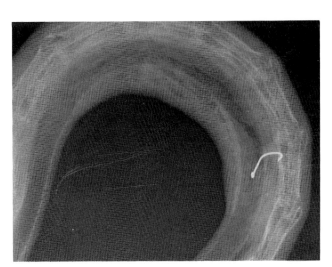
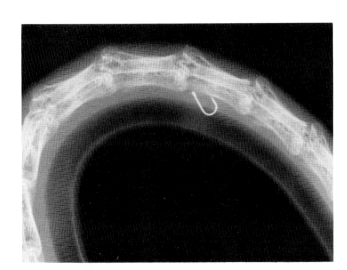
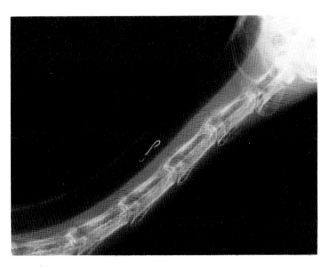

Typical X-rays.

Portsmouth family. Female is one day from death. Milton Common 21.5.88.

The Cob would now have to bring the Cygnets up alone.

This female was hooked in a 'no fishing' area. The hook was embedded in her stomach. We were unable to rescue her in time to save her life. Chasing a Swan in this condition can, and has, sometimes caused even greater suffering.

The float, being dragged through the water by a panicking Swan will tear the stomach or throat more.

We left Portsmouth and returned the next day to recover her body from the water.

The hardest lesson to learn is when not *to rescue.*

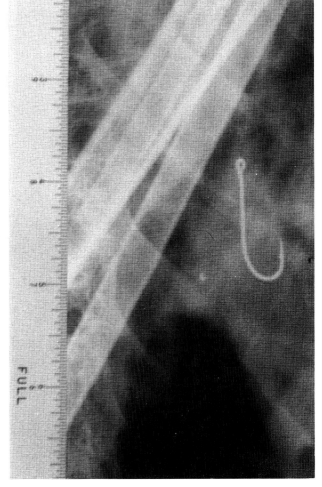

LEAD POISONING

Rollesby Broad, Norfolk. Already lead poisoned, not kinked neck. Now has hook in throat, line and more lead weights hanging. Swan died.

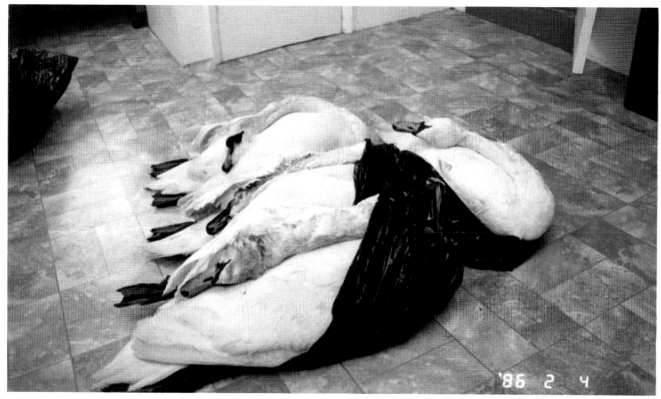

Lead poisoned Swans awaiting post mortem.

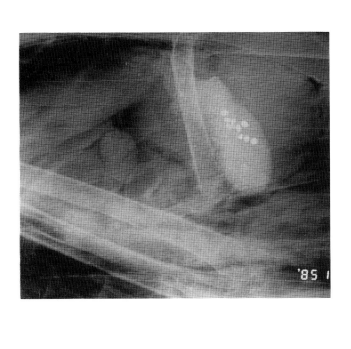
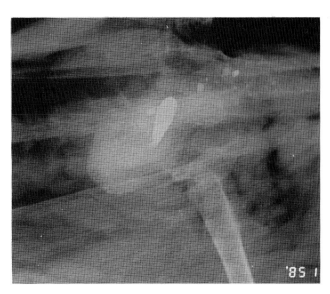

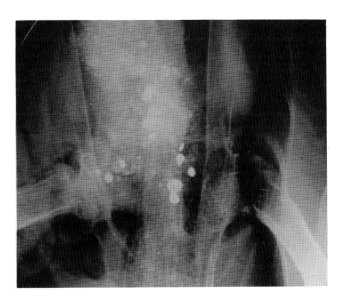
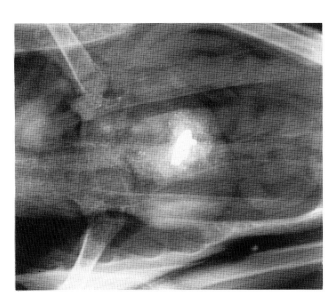

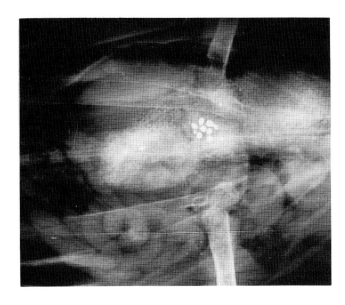
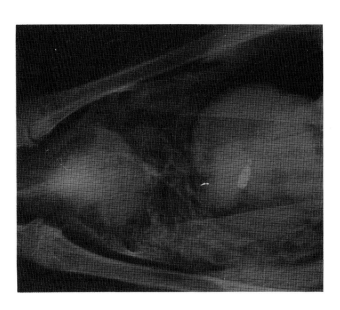

Typical X-rays showing lead in gizzards.

The problem with the authorities in Norfolk, in trying to get a piece of land for the Swans, continued. We tried everything we could. We now had so many disabled Swans in our care and were always afraid of a possible health risk. The control of disease being paramount, we used gallons of disinfectant, and continuing the way we had started, washed everything that was washable, pumped out ponds more than frequently and refilled them with fresh water. Food bowls were washed constantly and faeces disposed of. The problems with flies at times seemed insurmountable, especially when a Swan arrived bleeding profusely. Swans were therefore, after operations, kept inside the cottage, for fear of becoming fly blown and hence maggot infested.

We were, and went on to become, unpaid, unofficial and unrecognised, clearers up of the environment of Norfolk. When during low water and high temperature, Botulism swept through the population of waterbirds, upon the riverways and Broads, decimating whole groups of them, it was us that cleared up the bodies, in a futile attempt to abort the spread of this disease. The water authorities did not want to know.

We were more than disillusioned. Our letters of protest were still unanswered, and not even the successful selling of Pamela Townsend's book seemed to make a scrap of difference on the future fate of Britain's Swans. During the traumatic, but very necessary, promotion of the book, I had made many Broadcasts on radio and many television appearances. We were, with the Swans, eventually seen throughout the world. We had letters from everywhere. But still no help from the people of power, in our own country. I was offered a three month tour of California, but had to refuse, owing to the pressure of Swan work. The Americans could not believe that our nation of animal lovers could allow their Swans to be treated with such apathy. They wanted, and still do, the story of the Swan and the scandal of a nation that closed its eyes to the endeavours of our tiny band of rescuers.

Perhaps this book will help our American friends to see the truth.

That dichotomy that often arises when trying to publicise the plight of the Swan, is that the more publicity you receive, the more calls you get for Swans in distress. This I am afraid was the case with us. We were now sadly losing the battle. But what is more important, so were the Swans.

We had, again naively, thought that through embarrassment alone, the British Government would help us to save these noble creatures from a very dark fate. The story of lead poisoning, fishing tackle and power cables was now internationally known. But no help came. We continued our quest for the big white bird, but with not too much optimism.

During the autumn of 1982, the Swans were to receive another gift. Her name was Rina. Rina was to prove, to the Swans, their own Florence Nightingale. But more than that, was to become their sister and mother. Their friend and constant companion. She was brought to the cottage by a one time friend. She was quiet, timid and obviously at odds with what she considered an alien world, full of hurt and deceit. The only trust she never rejected, was the trust shown to her by animals. The only faith she seemed to possess, was directed, and indeed accepted by the animals. This trust and faith in animals was exacerbated by the failure of humans she had known to return her trust and faith, that she had naively, perhaps, placed in them. This outlook has never really changed, and the hurt and deceit shown by people to Rina was to be used against us all, at the Swan Rescue Service, for the coming years.

She had appeared at the cottage, looking for all the world like an escapee from an L. S. Lowry painting, wearing the expression of a frightened Fawn. She was small, slim and had stolen the tail from a wild plains Stallion, which she wore as hair. Rina had arrived. She had come to help with the Swans for a few weekends and is still here. As you will see.

There appeared in the classified advertisements section, of the local newspaper, an announcement that there was to be an auction of fifteen acres of marsh, in a village on the outskirts of Norwich, Costessey.

We contacted the auctioneer and enquired as to whether we could try to purchase the land before the auction. Getting the owner's telephone number we contacted him and were told the price. It was £22,000. The marsh had four hundred metres of river frontage and apart from its too close proximity to some houses, seemed ideal. The only thing that worried us was a power cable stretched across the river and the marsh. We thought, however, that the Electricity Board would, owing to the fact that we were running the only full time rescue service and Swan hospital, remove the cable and have it buried. That is what we thought. How wrong we were!

Being now so totally desperate for space for our Swans, we set about trying to raise the £22,000. I had cunningly kept most of the money earned from my French boat design contract and could raise nearly a half of the cost. A lady benefactor, who wishes to remain anonymous (from now on we shall refer to her simply as Swan Lady), would help us with the balance. We proceeded. Very soon the land was ours, or really the Swans, and we set about the erecting of fences and digging of ponds.

We were soon moving our disabled Swans down to their new home, at Costessey, and the marsh began to take shape. When finances permitted we employed a contractor to scoop out a lake. Eddie and Rina performed most of the tasks on the marsh that demanded strength and stamina. These qualities I was finding harder to use because of the reawakening of an old back injury, sustained whilst racing motor cycles, back in the "good old days" of civilisation. Whilst back at the cottage, welcoming incoming Swans, I was able to do more reading, when I could get the material, on the diseases of wild birds. I devoured any book I could find on blood, bones, diseases of heart, lungs, kidneys and liver. On ornithology, biology, and any other "ology" I could lay my hands on. As an ex London street kid, with an education grabbed between air raids, I found the studying more than difficult. It was difficult enough reading about the various diseases, but I could not pronounce them! What I had learned, in the damp interior of an air raid shelter, was of no use to me now. How to cheat at nine card brag would not help a Swan suffering from Aspergillosis. But I pressed on. I bought a cheap microscope and some slides, and a new, and very frightening, world opened up before me. I learned how to recognise Endoparasites, Ectoparasites and through the pages of *Blacks Veterinary Dictionary*, learned how to treat them. Although this famous dictionary obviously never included Swans, it was a matter of careful measurement of drugs and doses.

My microscope and I were now in the throes of a very deep love affair. I would cover her up at night time and when time permitted, gaze into her for hours discovering her secrets. After these long sessions, I would return to the kitchen, with an indentation around my right eye resembling a red rimmed monocle, blinking at the light and trying to focus on the teapot.

After my scientific journeys, through the eye piece of the microscope, I would bore Sheila, Eddie, Rina, the coalman and the milkman, with my tales of new microscopic discoveries. The overriding fascination that plagued me was that question that is probably asked by many ten year old children of average intelligence – what does the tiniest creature on the slide of the microscope eat? Then what does the creature that is eaten eat? And what does he eat? I had to put away my questions, and my microscope, for fear of losing my mind, but will always remember it with gratitude for helping to obtain some of the answers to our Swan problems. Especially the diagnosis of Aspergillosis.

In between the marsh work and Swan feeding at Costessey, Eddie and Rina formed a second rescue team, working together for a brief time. Paul and Sue Scheller having left amicably to get on with a normal lifestyle. They deserved it – they had saved many Swans and their dedication was appreciated by us all. We hope they found what they were looking for, we know that the Swans missed them.

The BBC had approached us with a view to make a half hour documentary on our work. You do not refuse the BBC, they are the best makers of Radio and Television documentaries in the world. This fact is derived through experience of other countries' attempts. We have experienced them. If the showing of a film would help better the chance of the Swan in obtaining help, the film just had to be made. The only stipulation made being that the BBC would not actually film us catching a Swan. This would encourage some of the cretins amongst us to carry out their perverted acts of cruelty.

We soon got used to the camera and sound crew following us around. Having a good basic training in stage craft during my youth whilst trying to become an actor, I was well used to the penetrating attention of an audience or the lens of a camera. The work went on. Dick Meadows' film, *The Dying Swan*, won the Royal Television Society award for documentary and was shown both on regional and national television, five times, apparently a record.

Instead of help, we received aggression. Aggression from anglers, shooters and, of course, the "Establishment". The people responsible through their negligence that had caused the deaths of thousands of Swans, by their procrastination in banning lead weights, were to say the least very embarrassed. Questions were asked "in the house" and red faced Ministers were questioned and had to find answers. Shortly after the film was shown the Nature Conservancy Council announced the ban on the import and sale of "certain sized" lead fishing weights. The decision obviously brought about not only by our film and our continual campaigning but also by the added weight of protests from the RSPB and the International Fund for Animal Welfare (IFAW). The use of lead weights now however needed further legislation. These papers pertaining to the banning of the use of lead weights were left within the in-trays of the offices of procrastination, inside the buildings of the Water Authorities, who were about to actually impose, and police their usage. This procedure took a further lengthy time to establish, meanwhile more Swans died. In 1987, January to be precise, "certain sized" lead weights were banned from sale by the NCC, the Water Authorities established the ban on their use at different dates throughout the British Isles. One Authority in the North East of England did not comply. No comment!

We wonder what will happen to these established bans on the use of lead, when privatisation of the Water Industry becomes finalised?

The stupidity of only banning certain sized lead fishing weights, is comparable to the stupidity of asking a human whether he would prefer to be shot by a small bullet or a larger one. Lead is lead. It is lethal, one of the deadliest of the heavy metals. This is a known fact. As a nation we have proved that we care, at least some of us, about the dangers to our children from inhaling lead from petrol fumes. Would it not be a better world also for our wildlife if they could enjoy a lead free environment?

The Swans had won a battle, but not the war. As retaliation for our campaigning success and the showing of our film, the threats started getting more frequent. We did not listen. Our cars were sabotaged and our rescue boat started to sink whilst Rina and I were trying to rescue a Swan. We got the Swan, and repaired the boat. The more scurrilous amongst the Angling tabloids attempted to conjure up stories, of their usual sensationalistic pap, about us, and amongst the fishermen and shooters of this "caring" little island, we were, for a time anyway, public enemy number one. The vomit printed by British tabloid newspapers can and indeed does destroy many people. If you are, however, a famous person, a pop star perhaps, you could afford a solicitor to fight the publishers and end up with a fortune, but more importantly, a retraction. You do not however stand a chance of a successful case against the pap publishers when you are working eighteen hours a day and possess a bank balance of thirty seven pounds fifty!

The thing that really galls us and really makes us want to give up our work, is that some of the people that had actually accepted these fictional statements in the papers, as fact, were indeed some of our supporters and helpers. This, as you can imagine, only helped to increase our trust in animals and decrease that trust in humans. Whether the reportage concerning you is true or untrue become of no consequence. The fact is, you have been mentioned in a tabloid newspaper. That stigma will be yours, to wear as a cloak of mistrust, for many a year. Meanwhile the grubby little journalist has long since gone on to other things of great national, and indeed international, importance. Like, for example, the fact that the girl who works behind the bar at the Coach and Horses has a seventy two inch bust and has recently had a liaison with the leader of the local train spotters society, who has a propensity to wear nothing but bifocal spectacles, one red plastic wellington boot and dipping the other foot in a bowl of cold custard, sings repeated choruses of the Marsellaise. (Whilst composing the above I came to the awful realisation that I could probably secure a well paid job on one of the tabloids!)

A sense of humour is the essential requirement if you are to live a life surrounded by death and destruction of those you love. It is merely a crutch to help prop up your slipping sanity.

The people that had refused to reply to our letters of protest now seemed to be suddenly aware of environmental issues. They could see electoral profits in adopting a "green" outlook. It had become trendy to be "green". But take comfort in the fact that there are people, not necessarily politicians, but ordinary people, who are taking up the challenge and are trying to do something to help our ailing planet. There is, thankfully, also a current trend amongst musicians and performers, to get involved in matters important to the environment. This can only be good for the environment.

Music is the universal language, it could prove to be the very vehicle for the transportation of ideas and ideals to a greater audience. This can only help recruit a new society of earth conscious, and environmentally aware, people. If it takes the interest, and consequently the efforts, of a well known and genuinely concerned young pop singer to spread the word about the destruction of a rain forest, then support that campaign. For within a simple song, or a television video, a message will be heard, seen and understood by thousands more people than populate the murky corridors of the parliamentary world. Let the politicians put the laws into proper form and push them through the slow process of parliament. But leave them, after you have made them aware of the problem, to do just that. It is the people who sincerely feel the sadness of the planet and its animals that can best speak for them. Politicians are the mechanics to continually service the machinery of power, by the well used lubrication of oratory.

Still the rescues continued. We now had over four hundred Swans living on their new marsh and to add to Rina's confusion and to the wheat bill, the free flying Swans had discovered our lake. This pleased us but not the people who lived close to the marsh. Complaints started. Swans are dangerous, they said. They would break your arms and were known to eat babies!

We were discovering that not many people really liked Swans. The people of Costessey were to become more vociferous with their complaints. We were, it seems, unpopular wherever we went with our Swans unless, of course, it was to rescue a Swan that had crash landed in one of their twee gardens or was a bloody, unsightly, badly injured Swan, that they wanted removing away from the sight of them and their children.

We were soon to discover a special breed of person who dwells within the villages and towns of the British Isles. They can be male or female, young or old. We had heard rumours, in the past, that they existed but had never encountered one. They are called "Parish Councillors". They appear, uninvited, at your door, or on your land, usually with clip board. The men have a habit of wearing tweed, the women twin sets, pearls and sensible walking shoes. They will, if you allow them, ask irrelevant questions and tick a piece of paper on their clip board when you reply. After telling you that you cannot do whatever it is that you want to do, they disappear mumbling that they have to report to a higher authority. These people carry power. They are guardians, at least in their own minds, of the establishment. They are, unfortunately, not an endangered species. There are many of them. Nobody knows where they come from. The majority that we have met, seem to prune roses, use slug bait and mind everybody else's business.

It is important that you never underestimate them, nor the power they possess, for they can, and do, turn upon you, with the speed and ferocity of a Viper. Especially if what you are doing, or what you have chosen to do is considered outside the "norm". Looking after the Swans of the British Isles, totally unaided by the establishment, is definitely outside the "norm".

If we had been called the "Royal" Swan Rescue Service, however, the above fact would not have applied.

So it was then, that the Costessey Parish Councillors trespassed onto our marsh, climbed over the closed and padlocked gate marked "Private No Entry" and clip boards at the ready, lumbered through the mud to face us. They told us that they did not think that it was right and proper to keep Swans on the marsh.

We agreed.

They told us that they had decided to complain to the County Council (the big boys) about the Swans, who had apparently brought thousands of rats and much danger to their village, and that they were a hazard and health risk.

We agreed.

They said that the Swans should be somewhere else and not so near to a village.

We agreed.

(With Parish Councillors always agree, they disappear far quicker if you do.)

They said it just was not right.

We agreed.

They said they also wanted the rights to walk along our riverbank, as they had done years ago.

We disagreed.

They went on. We walked away. They followed, this time using their well practised tone of obsequiousness, they are masters of this. They said that it was not them that disagreed with what we were doing but it was the people of the village. They indeed thought we were doing a good job and in fact supported us!

We agreed.

They went on to say that they did not think we should carry on our good work in their parish.

We agreed.

We asked if they knew of a place where we and the Swans would be left in peace. They did not know of a place, but surely there was one somewhere? We asked them if they knew of anybody who would buy us or give us such a place. They said they did not know.

We said we did not either.

They disappeared. But not for long. They pestered us all the while we had the misfortune to stay in the village. They are masters at the art of pestering. They have lots of questions but no answers.

Beware then of the Parish Councillor. He is the perfect citizen, the epitome of Englishness and the downright pain in the butt.

We all agreed.

The dark months of rescuing and burying our white friends slowly passed by and only the special magic moments kept our spirits buoyant enough to carry on. We increased our campaigning. We sent out quarterly newsletters informing our supporters of the progress so far with the new marsh. One day one of the magic moments came to us, as magic moments do, during a particularly depressing period.

Eddie had rescued a pair of Swans from the river at Lakenham, near Norwich. They were covered in diesel oil. Diesel oil is the worst form of pollution for a Swan, it is worse than crude oil. You cannot wash diesel from the feathers easily. Water when applied to a diesel oiled Swan, forms a wax, sticky mastic. The oil is then trapped between the water and the plumage and permeates the skin of the Swan. It has an acid action, the oil burning the skin.

In cases of diesel pollution, therefore, the treatment of choice is Fullers Earth, copiously applied and rubbed in as much as possible. The Fullers Earth will absorb some of the oil and the Swan will preen this now relatively harmless mess from his plumage. As with all oiled birds, the plumage damage must be treated after the most important part of bird, the insides are treated. We used Kaobiotic tablets always. A mixture of Kaolin and Antibiotics. These tablets were pushed down the bird's throat as soon as it was rescued. They would help to absorb ingested oil and take care of infection. If it is impossible to remove the oil, the Swan is kept in captivity until his next moult. When new feathers have replaced the oil damaged feathers, the Swan is then released.

For Swans arriving in the above condition, we had an especially small pen, so as to cut down take-off room, and lacking water. The Swans to remain as dry as possible. After their treatment Eddie put them in their pen. They were about seven years old and very friendly. They were obviously a devoted couple. They liked their pen and ate well, quite settled and satisfied. The pen they lived in was among the other four hundred Swans on the marsh, but this did not seem to bother them. The fence, around their pen, was made higher than other fencing, to make sure escape was impossible. For these Swans, to get back into water, would worsen their chances of a proper recovery.

One day the strong winds came. On windy days we were usually out attending power cable fatalities. This day was no exception. When we arrived back at the marsh, and made our usual check of the Swans, we were alarmed to discover that the male Swan of Eddies oiled pair had gone. Rina and Eddie searched the marsh but he was not to be found. His lady was obviously distressed. There was nothing we could do for her as she was not ready for release yet. We left her and went home. She remained in a state of depression, on her own in her pen. We knew that her mate's feathers were not good enough to sustain flight for very long and that he must be out there, somewhere, probably alone and pining. Yes, Swans do indeed pine when they have lost their mate. It was obviously the gale force winds that had taken him to premature freedom.

On a cold day, exactly six weeks after his disappearance, Rina was carrying out her morning Swan check, when her voice cut through the still air of the early morning.

"He's back, old Oily from Lakenham is back!" And sure enough he was. He was with his lady, in their pen, still with tattered feathers. He did not seem at all concerned. He offered us no explanation, but then no explanation was needed. He was after all a Swan, and Swans, as we all know cannot talk!

How he had found his lady, in her pen, in the middle of a flock of four hundred Swans, negotiated it from the sky and landed in an area of some eight foot by five foot, will remain a mystery.

In time the oily Swans became pure white Swans and were released back onto their old territorial river.

Showing effects of diesel oil on plumage.

CHAPTER 4
Of Myths, Magic and Fact

We have all heard the usual stories about Swans that tell of weird, mystical ways and spiritual prowess. Of human relationships and mythical beliefs. We will endeavour to put the record straight, or might indeed add to it.

Swans are very special people. Normally they do form a partnership for life but, after a while, some go their separate ways. Divorce is known and strange, humanlike relationships do occur.

An incident that moved me to tears, happened at a place called Loddon, on the River Chet, here in Norfolk. A Cygnet had been hooked after being caught in an unattended fishing line. In his panic he tore down river, pulling even more line from the reel on the fishing rod. By the time I had arrived the Cygnet had gone. Just Dad was there, he was very agitated and was rushing from one side of the river to the other, creating great bow waves and slapping at the surface of the water with his wings. He was very annoyed. His lady and the other four Cygnets stayed well clear of him and sat quite still some way off.

He saw me, swam directly toward me, then in an instant abruptly changed direction and, turning sharply, headed up river. Swimming at an alarming speed he shot around the bend in the river and again started beating the water with his wings, sending great splashes of spray upwards. Then the Cygnet appeared. His tiny body was part submerged. The fishing line had entangled both legs and then around his scrawny, still short neck, holding it down partly beneath the surface of the water. There were metres of line and a float trailing behind him. I reached toward the baby but had no chance of putting my Swan hook around his pipe cleaner like, waterlogged, little neck.

Then Dad attacked. He leapt towards his offspring and seemed to be attacking the Cygnet's rear end, snapping with his great orange beak. He then turned within his own space and swam away from the tiny, squeaking creature. I was amazed to see that Dad had the fishing line in his beak, as he shot past me very close to the bank. The baby, now being towed, beached upon the shallow mud. I had him. Dad watched, and with trembling hands I disentangled his Cygnet, took the hook from the thigh muscle and placed the baby back into the water. As soon as the Cygnet was safely back with his Dad, so Dad attacked me. But his wings never made contact. They swam off together.

Accident?

Happenstance?

Probably. But true.

A long time ago, when financially, things were very tight, I decided to sell my collection of long playing records to buy petrol for the Swan car. This was a very hard thing to do, as I have mentioned, but necessary. Looking through them for the last time, I had noticed a beautiful picture on one of the sleeves. A magnificent Swan. The record was Wagners, Lohengrin. The Swan on the record sleeve looked very much like a beautiful Cob Swan I knew on the River Bure at Coltishall, in Norfolk. He had a lady who, through an old injury, had received a fish hook scar from the rear of her beak to above her ear. This scar gave the impression that she was perpetually smiling. We called her "Grin" and her husband "Loh" and thanked Mr Wagner!

Thousands of miles away and two years before we started our Swan Rescue Service, someone else had christened a pair of Swans, Loh and Grin. That someone also wrote something called, *On the Waterfront*, the Oscar winning film starring Marlon Brando. The writer of the screenplay was Budd Schulberg. Budd had also written a book called *Swan Watch*, telling of the lives of his Loh and Grin. Two years then, after we had named our Swans, the book, quite by accident, came into our possession. It was amongst a pile of other books bought cheaply from a sell out at a local library.

Years later, Rina and I were to share dinner with Budd Schulberg, at his house on the banks of the Aspatuck river, on Long Island, New York. The spirit of Loh and Grin, long since departed, was still there. Thankyou, Budd.

Loh and Grin. England.

Rina and I were called to an area of Suffolk that has always worried us – just up the road from Sizewell Nuclear Power Station. We had been told that there was a family of dead Swans, floating on a dyke. A whole family, all dead, obviously needed investigating. We searched the marshes for some time and then we saw them. They were lying in green algae covered water. The mother and her five brand new babies were lying together. There was no sign of the Cob.

We made our way slowly over a series of dykes and through the marshes to the family. As we were photographing this pathetic scene, we heard the familiar sound of a Swan's wings. The Cob flew low over our heads and circled, watching the scene below. We left his family in their water. We knew, by bitter experience, that there was no point in our recovering the bodies. We had lost Swans in this area before, and never, ever, were able to get Ministry results, after giving them the dead Swans. They, in fact, seemed to "lose" these bodies from around Nuclear Power Stations.

As we were leaving the marshes the Cob landed and stood upon the bankside, overlooking his family and watched us until we drove away.

We obviously never discovered the reason for his family's deaths, but then again we were not meant to.

The Cob knew we had been.

A milkman had called us early one spring morning to say he had seen a dead Swan beneath a power cable. He was not sure whether another Swan, standing close to the dead Swan, was injured. I set out alone, as Rina, Sheila and Eddie were at this time working on an incoming Swan. The cable run was not far from the centre of Norwich. We knew it well, it was situated on the marshes in a place called Whittlingham Lane. There is no sky here, just power cables.

When I arrived I saw the white shapes through the binoculars. One Swan was definitely dead, but I was not sure about the other. I climbed the marsh fence and made my way to this sad, so familiar, scene. It was indeed a pitiful sight. The female had mercifully been killed instantly and her mate had landed, to be with her. He was now sitting next to her pure white, stretched out, body. The whiteness now spoiled by the revolting burns across her chest. He stood, as I approached, but did not move away. I spoke to him, while I put his mate in the black plastic sack I always carried and he just stood there, watching, just one foot away from me.

As soon as I had covered her head, however, he started running, to achieve take-off speed. He lifted high, just missing other cables, circled once and disappeared over the River Yare.

His lady was safe.

I took her home.

When the Swans lived with us at the cottage they would suddenly stop whatever they were doing and, with necks straight up and heads pointing to the sky, stand perfectly still, as if they were frozen into stark, white statues. This would not last long and, within a few seconds, they would carry on about their business preening, eating, whatever.

This strange occurrence would fascinate us and, when time allowed, we would rush around to see if anyone was about.

On one winter Wednesday morning, we were to find out why the Swans behaved this way. Wednesday was the day of the local shoot. The peasants, accompanied by the Vicar, were walking, with shot guns broken across their waxed cotton covered shoulders, down the lane, through the snow on their way to the killing fields, after the unfortunate imported Asian Chicken – the Pheasant.

The Swans knew.

Do we tend to read more than is true, when we live with wildlife? Are we guilty of gross anthropomorphism?

Probably. But we saw these things, and we were not alone.

A "bird person" we knew admitted to us that he could not work with Swans because he was afraid of becoming too involved with them. He was right. They have a way about them. They can, and they do, take your every moment. To sit amongst a flock of Swans is, for us, the perfect treatment to alleviate the stresses brought about by our modern society. To experience pure truth and loyalty, is a gift not often found when with most human beings. We are too full of complexities and vagueness, of worries, doubts and anxieties. A Swan is simply a Swan.

We wear confusion, as he wears feathers.

A myth that prevails, to this day, is that all Swans belong to the Queen. This is not so. The exception being the Swans that live upon the River Thames. These are, by tradition, owned equally by the Worshipful Company of Dyers and the Worshipful Company of Vintners and the Crown – or supposed to be. That is when in recent "dark" days, the poor Swans were pinioned, to ensure that they would not leave the Thames. This butchery being carried out by the Dyers' and Vintners' labourers and the Royal Swan keepers. We believe this pinioning has ceased altogether upon the River Thames. We only hope, for the sake of the perpetrators, that it has.

We have already explained the plight of the Mute Swan in the British Isles. Because of total lack of compassionate management he is, and always will be, suffering. Imagine then the incongruity of the barbaric and totally unnecessary annual "bean feast" known as "Swan Upping".

The fact that all Swans now, upon the River Thames, are full winged and, in fact, apart from a few pairs, are flocks of non breeding Swans, flying in from the many reservoirs and gravel pits that surround the river, obviously negates ownership – be it by the Dyers, Vintners or the Crown. These are free, wild Swans. But this obviously well known fact would interfere with a typical British excuse of having a good day out on the river.

Swan Upping is a throwback from the days of Bear baiting and Dog fighting. It still goes on every July, when overgrown schoolboys, usually inebriated, bedecked in antique uniforms, invade the river with

Picture: Paul Felix.

smart, equally antique, barges, displaying heraldic banners and persecute Swans.

It is one of the most anachronistic and cruel traditions still carried on by loyalists and decent "right thinking" pillars of British society.

Swan Upping is, as far as we are concerned, a miscarriage from the rapidly developing womb of animal welfare awareness. It is an anathema.

The hooligans chase the Swans, surround them in their little boats, pull the Cygnets, already terrified by the chase, from the water by their necks and, using a pen knife, cut into the still rubbery, tiny beaks, to make their marks of ownership. A special mark for the Dyers, a special mark for the Vintners and unmarked Swans for the Queen. Imagine the stress caused to these innocent birds. The Swan families are then divided into thirds, each family being kept, as much as possible, complete. After about a fortnight of this game, many Swans upon the River Thames are suffering stress. We do not know how many Cygnets die, or how many families are split up. We cannot

imagine that drunken schoolboys could get this right! The photographs accompanying this text make this graphic, more than words can explain.

When we have, in the past, protested about this barbarism, we have been told by scientists from Oxford University, that Swan Upping was of great significance in the gaining of information on the effects of lead poisoning. But this obviously would be the case if you were receiving grants from the various "supposed" Swan owners. The attitude shown by the scientists can be compared with the same attitude shown by countries still harpooning Whales for "scientific reasons".

These same scientists were responsible for removing Swans from the River Thames, many of the Swans already weakened by the effects of lead poisoning, taking up to ten millilitres of blood and putting the Swan straight back into the water. So much for scientists!

We recovered some of these moribund Swans later.

Vandalism perpetrated in the name of tradition. River Thames.

Swans are categorised, under the Wildlife and Countryside act, as wild birds. They have, however, no special protection. Prosecutions, therefore, are very difficult to obtain against people who, even knowingly perpetrate cruelty. To instigate stress is an act of cruelty. We have, upon post mortem, seen the manifestation of stress induced death. A disease, known as Amyloidosis, is thought to be caused by stress (Cowan and Johnson, 1970). The post mortems carried out by us and the Ministry of Agriculture, where Amyloidosis was found, were from Swans known to have suffered stressful injuries or had suffered prolonged captivity in overcrowded conditions. Wild birds so often handled by the inexperienced can also succumb to Amyloidosis. Power cable collisions, and victims of leg ringing also, it has been proven, suffer from the disease. Therefore, to instigate stress can only be construed as cruelty. Academic cruelty, if you will, but cruelty none the less.

There is a lot of cruelty, going unpunished, upon the River Thames every July.

Cutting Cygnets beak, no veterinary training, no anaesthetic, no feeling, no sense, no reason, Swan "Uppers" enjoying their day out.

Picture: Paul Felix.

The question most often asked us is, perhaps, not a surprising one. How big was the biggest Swan you ever saw? The answer must be a dear old gentleman reputedly some twelve years of age. We called him Zeus. He had an incredibly gentle disposition, and would often leave his water to visit a riverside shop to scrounge for bread. He never, during the four years we knew him, had a mate. We had to rescue him three times. Because this kindly old Swan trusted all humans, he could not differentiate between the well meaning human with a loaf of bread, and the fisherman with his bread bait. So he would unfortunately swim towards the fisherman and his line. All rescues were to extricate fish hooks.

The first time I pulled him from the water was, indeed, a terrible shock. I had never lifted such a heavy Swan. Because of the extent of surgery required to take out one of the fish hooks, I had occasion to take the old chap home for a couple of days. After he had undergone his operation and was once more returned to his old state of friendliness, so was approachable, I took the opportunity of noting some of his vital statistics. From the back of his neck, to the very tip of his tail, measured forty nine inches. His weight was exactly eighteen kilograms (approx. thirty eight pounds). But the most amazing statistic of all, was his wing span, exactly nine foot four and a half inches.

This wonderful old Swan was to leave us, early one spring, when a plebeian in a motor boat reversed into him and he was cut to pieces by the propeller. He died, with us, at the cottage, and is buried there. The only reminder of Zeus being two fencing stakes I had placed in the garden, at exactly nine foot four and a half inches apart.

The other myth, one in fact that annoys us, is that Swans are aggressive creatures. He is aggressive obviously if you attempt to interfere with his offspring. The same, I hope, as you or I. It is an act of gross stupidity to approach a nesting Swan for purposes of photography or study, for example.

Bird ringers usually feel the worst of the Swan's aggression when the idiots attempt to ring Cygnets who are, in any case, far too young to ring. It's a pity that the male Mute Swan is not really as aggressive as he is made out to be! We could do with a lot less bird ringers, in fact the ideal number of bird ringers, disturbing and stressing birds, would be nil!

After rescuing and treating some seven thousand Swans, we have only ever experienced one Swan that really just did not like people. She was known by us as "Vicious Cow". She lived at Martham, upon the river Thurne. Her neck was strangely bent, this being the result of an attack by a canoeist who had, because the Swan was on his river, hit out at her with his oar. This, then, probably planted within this Swan the seed of aggression. Two vertebrae in her neck had been displaced, so had set crooked.

She was hooked, one day in late summer, and we set off to find her. This was not difficult, she was already coming down river looking for us! She met us with wings up and neck right back. At least, as far as

it would go. We did not catch her, we seemed to be wearing her!

The hook was deeply embedded in her oesophagus so we had to take her to our trusty vet for the operation. He used twice the normal amount of anaesthetic to render the old lady unconscious. Apparently the dose required for this being average for an Alsatian Dog. To work on this Swan can only be compared to trying to control Hurricane Hugo with your cupped hands. She was then, as you can imagine, a fighter!

Her operation went very well and soon the one inch hook was out. We took her back to the stable pen and left her to come round from the effects of the anaesthetic. After attending to other Swans, a couple of hours later, Sheila took a food bowl over to the stable pen.

The crash from somewhere inside the stable, sending clouds of dust through the shaft of sunlight entering the open door, signalled, in no uncertain way, that Vicious Cow had come to. Sheila's head momentarily came into view over the lower stable door, looking for a split second like the other half of a Punch and Judy show. Punch, though, was not seen! This episode being reminiscent of the classic Parkinson and Emu interview on BBC TV.

I covered the distance from the back of the cottage to the stable, at a speed that can only be described as Olympic standard, and found that Sheila was on her knees, looking up to Vicious Cow. Sheila, when standing, is exactly five foot tall, which means that when facing an average adult Mute Swan, with the Swan at full stretch, its beak is roughly as high as her nose. When, however, you are kneeling on the floor, the Swan could be twenty five foot tall, Vicious Cow was now sixty two foot tall! The food bowl, now devoid of food, was still in Sheila's left hand and Vicious Cow, old newspaper, Swan faeces, and feathers, were in her right hand, on her head and on her body, in fact, the only way Sheila was recognisable, was by her slightly Welsh accent. This vocal noise was more of a shriek crossed with hysterical laughter. I joined the fight, and tried to grab Vicious Cow. Now this Swan, among other things, is definitely not grabbable. A sear pain shot up my left leg. Her very accurate beak had found, precisely, that secret part of a human anatomy that is ever so slightly below the groin, above the knee, to the inside of the thigh, that "brings tears to the eyes" place! At the same time, this dear old Swan, slapped both my legs with her wings. Through the tears I could see that Sheila, now making a noise resembling an uncontrollable Celtic giggle, or long forgotten war chant, was heading towards the cottage. I could not leave the stable, however, so spent a few seconds, or what seemed like hours, crying, indeed screaming, in pain. There seemed nothing more constructive to do.

It took three days to finally get Vicious Cow eating again. When her stitches were out she was released (I'm not too ashamed to admit) by Eddie, back onto her river.

The next time, however, we were to meet Vicious

Cow was two years later, when Eddie brought her home, in a plastic sack. The only humans she never got the better of, were the humans that had put a thirty two thousand volt power cable alongside her river.

We loved her immensely, and we miss her terribly.

Swans then are as aggressive as you or I would be should we find an intruder in our own home, about to do harm to our loved ones. So be it with the Swan. Breeding Swans are, of course, territorial. Their space is precious to them. Normally, when on a river, they will need about a mile long stretch of water. This area, if adequate water vegetation is present, is needed to bring up their family successfully. If, as unfortunately, in this day and age their stretch of river is a concrete sided canal, or such like, then they only have the food offered by humans to sustain them and their family. This is when trouble usually breaks out. Breeding Swans will patrol their waters constantly just prior to, and during, breeding and raising their families. Should another Swan cross the invisible, to us, territorial line, then he is in trouble.

The male, usually, of the established breeding pair, will chase and attack the intruder until he leaves the territory. If he refuses to leave then the battle usually follows, the intruding Swan, more often than not, coming off worse. In some cases, though rare, the established male will kill the intruder, this we stress, is very rare. The exception to the rule, however, being when the poor intruder is weak or sick and begging for food. We have known of Swans terribly injured through power cable collisions, and still dazed, landing in other Swans territories. In these situations it can be counted as a blessing should the crippled, bleeding victim be given ultimate peace by one of his own kind.

Swans kill by holding their victim's head beneath the water, resulting in drowning. This is, let us not forget, less traumatic and far more merciful than catching the injured Swan and driving him many miles to a veterinary surgeon to be put to sleep by injection.

It is a pity that a certain inspector, working for a large animal welfare organisation and stationed in

Leicester, some time ago, was not capable of understanding wildlife. When called by a riverside pub and told that the male Swan, of a territorial pair, was acting aggressively and scaring his clientele, the inspector, being a trigger happy, pseudo "Dirty Harry", blasted the Swan to death with a rifle. The Swan was being a Swan, the inspector was out of order and the female had to bring the family up, all alone.

The reason for this Swan's continual displays of what the onlookers considered aggressive, was that, owing to riverside development and boating all of the Swan's natural foodstuff had been destroyed. He had only the crisp wielding pub customers to rely on for food. We were told by supporters, from Leicestershire, that this was not the only time this had happened. Indeed, later on, we were to witness the appalling actions of a group of animal welfare people shooting hundreds of Swans.

If a breeding pair are unfortunate enough to nest upon a small lake, or worse still a village pond, they will endeavour to rid that pond of every other waterbird, so as to ensure they are of no threat to their own future offspring. They will trample Ducks, Ducklings, Goslings and other small waterbirds beneath the water. This, in a human's terms, is aggression. To an animal's instinct, however, it is survival. This instinct is brought about by thirty million years of evolution. A pseudo animal lover will panic and call us to travel to their village pond and get rid of these "nasty, aggressive, evil Swans". When we try to explain that not only is it illegal to remove an uninjured wild bird, but also, in our opinion, immoral, the caller will accuse us of not caring! You cannot please all the people all of the time. If a Swan is killing a Swan or a Duck or Goose, we will not interfere. The only exception, of course, being when Man has caused, through stupidity or mismanagement, this situation to prevail. Usually the situation is instigated by a well meaning, but unthinking, member of the village community that wants "pretty birds" on his village pond. By excessive feeding of village pond birds, ordinary, innocent, well meaning people encourage waterbirds to inhabit an area of water only large enough for either a pair of Swans or a group of small birds, but not both. To the minds of some of these people, aesthetics are all important, and the understanding of wildlife irrelevant. We are called to clear up his mistakes. At least we were.

The Swan will also kill his own offspring. We have witnessed this several times. We have never interfered and always considered this "Swans business". But on occasions we did remove the little carcasses and have them post mortemed. On every occasion the post mortem examination revealed that the Cygnet was suffering terminal illness, either disease or lead poisoning (typically lead ions passed through a lead poisoned mother into the yoke of the egg). In all cases the Swans knew better than we that their own offspring were suffering. Also, with even modern drugs at our disposal to enable us to end the suffering of a sick, very small Cygnet, it could not have been more humane, or more natural, than to have left the Cob (male Swan) to do the job. It takes the Cob about ten seconds of holding his baby's head beneath the water, to give it peace. It would take us longer than that to find the Cygnet.

Swans and, indeed, wild Geese, with us for treatment, would show us who amongst other birds in care, were beyond help. They would try, and sometimes succeed, to end their suffering. We should have the strength, although this is difficult, to watch and learn this very important lesson, brought about through the teacher of evolution. We tend to believe that because we can read, write, and digest text books, that we know better than the animal. We do not. An amazing fact that unfolded during some of these instinctive displays – the Geese and Swans that tried to kill other birds in our care, did not, much to our surprise, pick upon those birds that had obvious, visible injuries, broken wings, legs etc., but would try to kill birds that to us seemed reasonably fit, outwardly anyway. How did they know? This would happen at home with birds in our care and outside on rivers and marshes. Every bird that was killed by another bird was proven, through post mortem examination, to be suffering chronic illness or internal injury. Unknown by us but somehow known by a creature of the wild. What would we give to have our doctors blessed with this very special gift?

A very long time ago, in a different country, a respected old man once said, "If you need to understand a Swan, then become one." For three days, with arms flapping at 2.7 beats per second, I ran up and down the road, outside the cottage and, when I thought I had attained sufficient speed, hopped at every five paces. Nothing happened. On the third morning the nurse at the hospital checked my chart at the foot of the bed and told me I could now go home. On my way home I called in at the dairy, to apologise to our milkman for landing amongst his Gold Tops and farm fresh butter. He was still at the dairy, owing to the fact that it was difficult delivering milk with both arms in slings and a size eight Dunlop wellington boot jammed in an unmentionable part of his anatomy. I gave up my attempts at flying without power, like a Swan, however, when further learning taught me that to achieve sufficient thrust for take-off, when you are blessed with the power to weight ratio of a Swan, you would need to be able to lift off the ground whilst carrying a grand piano under each arm. I gave up my flying attempts, not because of lack of confidence, but because I could not afford two grand pianos.

What I think, in retrospect, the old man meant was that you had to live with Swans to understand them, and living with them was a continual source of amazement to us all. We never tired of their company and at times were hysterical when watching their antics. They are the only birds we know that actually played games. A favourite game, for some of our young Swans, was "the throwing the stone game". This consisted of picking nice round stones from the aggregate, surrounding their ponds, lifting them with their beaks and then with a flick of the head, sending the stones up and away from them. The "click clacking" of pebbles falling on pebbles would go on for ages and, when a stone landed on the back of a sleeping Swan, the look of surprise from that Swan was very comical.

When the sun appeared upon the water, usually on early spring mornings, with the Swans contentedly going about their Swan business, one Swan would start, without warning, the "circle" game. He would start off by swimming at an incredible speed, wings flapping the water, and tear round the pond at increasing circumferences. Immediately other Swans would copy, so that the pond would become a boiling, bubbling mass of waves and rainbow water droplets, which with the whiteness of the Swans and the silver water, was sometimes too dazzling to watch.

The older, more stately, Swans would leave the water to the younger ones and stand on their bank watching them play, with the disinterest of over-dressed matrons, surveying their charges enjoying themselves in a seaside hotel swimming pool. As suddenly as the "circle" game had started, it would stop, the water again finding its proper level and the youngsters would preen in the spring sun. All was right with the world.

A game that was enjoyed by all was the "banging of the bucket handle" game. When we were using buckets to feed the Swans, we obtained those with the wire and wooden handles. The wooden handgrip spun on the wire hoop. These handles would keep the Swans amused for hours. They would lift the handle with their beak and enjoy the crack, when released, of the hand grip slapping the side of the bucket. As the wooden handle revolved, it was difficult for the Swan to hold it, so it would spin, at every attempt, upon its wire axle. Some of the stronger, bigger Swans would stop this game by grabbing the handle of the bucket, pulling the whole thing over and, without a word, shuffle off. The ever present small furry creatures, with long tails, would enjoy this, and the resident Pheasant would, after dusk, be seen clearing up the wheat with his tiny rodent friends helping.

The game of "bashing the window at the cottage for food" was discouraged, however, owing to the danger of broken glass to the Swans.

There was one lady Swan, called Mrs Fuller, who stole the coffee from my mug, while I was concentrating on chipping the Swans' potatoes. An excited cry from Rina called me to survey a very strange scene. Mrs Fuller, looking very guilty, with coffee dripping from her orange beak, had found a new and interesting taste. She would, in future, seek out my coffee mug for her illicit drinking spree, but we did not encourage this. Well, not really!

Swans choose their life partners, much the same as we do. This fact is, unfortunately, not understood by the many people who have asked us to supply a mate for a bereaved Swan – you do not. A recent case concerned a very old Swan friend of ours who lost his lady, he had been with her for a long time. We were asked by the people, who we had given him to (for prolonged care), for another mate. We tried to explain that Swans choose their mates, but they were gently adamant and very insistent. We, after much discussion, relented. It was a total disaster. The poor little female was chased out of the water by the male and had we not been there he would very likely have killed her. It was our usual practice to bring a bereaved Swan back to our sanctuary, to choose their own mate. But on this occasion it was not possible. We had to take the terrified female back home. Like some humans, some Swans are perfectly content to be alone, but humans always seem to imagine Swans should be in pairs. Not learning from this terrible experience, however, the guardians of the male Swan enquired as to where they might obtain another, different, female!

Swans are not objects of adornment for lakes and ponds. They are individual beings with their own patterns of behaviour, their own quirks and their own individuality. Just as we are. It is very difficult to get people to understand this.

They are not, and never have been, "our Swans".

But we are "their people".

We have met many old bachelor Swans and many old spinster Swans, who are perfectly content to be on their own. Simply "being" is enough, for the Swans at least.

"The Deva" was the oldest Swan we ever knew. We rescued her, in a weak and run down condition, from North Wales. She had suffered a wing injury and was now too old to keep up with the stronger, much younger, Swans who lived in the harbour. She could not compete for food. It was time for the old lady to go into retirement. We brought her home. She had been ringed forty years before her rescue and stayed with us until she was forty four. Reliable information, provided by a delightful old trawlerman, told us her story. She had been with her mate for a very long time but he left some five years earlier her rescue. He had died of old age, it was thought. He simply, according to our old Welsh friend, put his head upon his back and went to sleep. The sea took him and his dreams away from the harbour and his lady. The only "proper" Swan death we have ever known. The Deva was never interested in any other Swan. She was simply content to "be".

Loneliness then is a concept, a feeling, that is experienced by many humans. What right have we to believe that it is experienced and suffered by a Swan. We think that the Swan knows best. We have to accept this fact. He, the Swan, anyway, has shown us this is true.

CHAPTER 5
Another Move

After seven years of struggle, pain and frustration, we still had not been offered any help from either the Government, or the various trusts concerned with the environment. We had made a, what turned out to be, terrible mistake in becoming a Registered Charity.

The only help we were to receive, financially, apart from continued support from our Newsletter readers, was from Brian Davies and Ian McPhail of the International Fund for Animal Welfare (IFAW). They supplied enough money for us to purchase a better Swan ambulance and a much needed Endoscope, to help us in the surgery. But the greatest gift they gave us, and the Swans, was continual campaigning to obtain a ban on the use of lead fishing weights. Apparently Mrs Thatcher received some 60,000 postcards of protest sent by IFAW members. Also, they helped us, and are continuing to help us, and you, by relentless campaigns for all the other animals in the world of suffering. We, and the Swans, thank them, so do the other animals.

My health had now deteriorated considerably. An active seven years, spent in the cold and dampness of Norfolk, worsening the problem with my back. We would return from river and marsh rescues soaking wet, and carry on with new rescues, wearing the same clothes. The new rescue could be any distance away, from ten miles to two hundred. We never had time to change our clothes, the injured Swan requiring immediate attention. His treatment was a matter of life and death, our problem was that of discomfort. The Swan came first. We have, however, paid for this lack of self consideration since. Our tiny team were now covering up to two thousand miles a week over the highways and byways of the British Isles.

The long, dormant seed of discontent planted in the minds of the people of Costessey, by the Parish Councillors, and fertilised by the manure of gossip, was now flowering into a healthy bloom of hatred and resentment. The Swans, and us, were still not wanted. But we had nowhere to go. The only light at the end of the tunnel, was that our Swan Lady, our benefactor, had told us that if ever we saw a place, the right place, a larger house with land, then she would buy it for us and the Swans. We looked everywhere.

Because of the continual problem of the power cable over our marsh at Costessey, we had had to release all except the disabled Swans, but there were about two hundred of the poor creatures.

Back at the cottage, at Sparham, Sheila would buy the local newspaper every day and scour the property advertisements. During this transient period Rina was taken seriously ill, and the ever prevailing evil at Costessey marsh manifested itself in no uncertain manner, as will be explained by Rina, later. It is her story and it is the Swans wish that she should tell it.

When the trees of autumn were wearing their new coats of russet and gold, when leaves crunched under foot, like a million cornflakes, and when depression was sifting through to our souls, we found the place.

It was an old, rambling farmhouse, deep within the Norfolk countryside, yet only seven miles from Norwich. It had an old pond. Silted up and quite small, but a pond never the less. It had nearly two acres of land, but within the house there were sufficient rooms to convert to surgery and operating theatre, oiled Swan bathroom, offices, studio/darkroom and enough room left for us. It was unmodernised and needed a lot of work, and a lot of money, to make it suitable for Swans. They would have the heating and comfort, we would have what they did not want. In fact our small part of the house was comparable to living in a wind tunnel at times, but we would have first choice amongst the jumble, given to raise money for the Swans, to select jumpers and cardigans. This to us seemed cheaper than the installation of proper heating. If we were that cold, we could always share the surgery with the Swans!

Our Swan Lady bought the house and Sheila and Eddie started the unenviable process of moving everything from the old cottage to the new Swan Rescue Service headquarters, at Lathe Green Farm, Shotesham St Mary. Rina and I set about making Lathe Green into a Swan hospital and a hospice. The farmhouse was isolated and peaceful. The only other buildings nearby were delapidated barns, dairy and stables, to the side of the house. These were owned by a local farmer.

Obviously the first job for Rina and I, was to restore the old pond. This was not as easy as we had thought. As I have mentioned, Rina is of slight build and weighs about eight stone, I am middle aged, awkward and useless at heavy physical work. The most excruciating task for a back sufferer to perform, is using a shovel. We had lots of shovelling to do. We loaded over seventy wheelbarrows full of black silt. Pushing each barrow over to the back of the land, some hundred and twenty metres away, each barrow seeming heavier than the last. Whenever we were out and about on rescues, we would meet muscle bound men who would offer us any physical help we needed. When called on for such help, however, they were always either away on holiday, or were suffering back troubles! We carried on, as usual, alone. We even applied to the local Government offices dealing with the thousands of unemployed, seeking manual work. They did, in fact, send a couple of people. The hardest, most physically demanding work they had ever done, however, seemed to be the turning or pushing of a knob on a television set, or opening their Giro envelope. They left.

Unable to walk properly after our excursions with the wheelbarrows, we decided to call it a day. We consulted the local Yellow Pages. There must be people who specialise in the clearing of ponds and, sure enough, we found one such firm.

They said they would send their technical representative. She arrived the next day, with her clip board, "tut tutted" twice and said she would arrange a quotation. We had no choice any way, but to accept the quotation, theirs being the only company, locally, that had the necessary equipment.

The man came, clad in blue overalls and total disinterest, surveyed the pond and immediately took up his "negative" stance. This is easily recognisable by the student of body language. Feet slightly apart, both hands thrust into pockets, he studied our "would-be Swan lake" and slowly, shaking his head from side to side, muttered the oft used expression of the disinterested and completely negative, "roll on Friday brigade".

"Dear, dear."

"What's the matter?" we said.

"Oh dear, oh dear," he replied.

"Can you do it?" we asked.

"Dunno," he replied.

Rina and I looked at each other with that "we have a right Wally here" expression. The intellectual one continued.

"There's a lot of it," he said.

"We know," we replied.

"Well I dunno," he said.

"You don't know what?" we said.

"Well, sort of thick init," he asked. Rina politely stopped herself from saying the obvious. Rina is a lady.

"Well, yes," we simply replied.

"You got a right bloody problem 'ere," he said.

"We know," we replied.

Without taking his hands from his pockets, he suddenly burst into alarming action. He slowly swung his right leg and nonchalantly kicked a small pebble into the water. It sort of just lay there, on the surface. It didn't sink.

"Oh dear, oh dear, oh dear, oh dear," Mastermind said.

Rina and I left him to get on with our work. About a quarter of an hour later, our man shouted.

"Right then," he said.

We wandered slowly towards him, wondering what great discovery our man of technology had made.

"Pardon?" we said.

"Righto then," he replied.

"Righto then what?" we asked. Without answering he disappeared out of the side exit to the pond and we waited. We heard the diesel engine of the "sludge gulper" burst into life and soon it appeared – a great

blue creature, with a long black trunk. Our man unwound the trunk and put the end of it beneath the surface of the black silt. Using some strange voiceless command, he ordered the creature to start sucking. So suck it did. Great gulps of black sludge were taken down the trunk to the creature's blue, steel stomach. Pretty soon we could see black water appearing, where there had only been black silt. The creature continued to drink and, within half an hour, it appeared to have had enough. It stopped drinking.

"That's it," said the man.

"That's what?" we asked.

"Time's up," he said.

"What do you mean?" we queried.

"Arf past four," he said.

"We know," we replied.

"I'm orf then, see you in the morning," he said. On another command from him the creature, changing the pitch of its voice, started to wind its trunk in. It then, with its master in control, reversed awkwardly down the old farm drive, making funny gurgling sounds from its stomach, as the black silt splashed about inside.

He never came back. We could not afford him and his big blue creature. Rina and I went back to shovels, wheelbarrows and pain.

A week or so later, we decided that enough black silt had been removed. We now had some water, black, but water never the less. We put our little submersible electric pump into the black water and dragged its hose down to the front of the house into the drainage ditch. We intended to drain dirty water from the pond, whilst filling with clean water.

It was on the second day of pumping the water into the drain, that He arrived. He was red faced, young, flustered and out of breath.

"Stop that pump!" he ordered.

"Who the hell are you?" we asked.

"Anglian Water," he replied. He went on.

"You are pumping dirty water into the drainage ditch, and the water is going down to the brook, and Mr Hamers' cows are drinking the water and dirty water is poisonous, and his cows could suffer and anyway, its illegal."

"What's illegal?" we enquired.

"Pumping dirty water into a waterway," he said.

"But its a drain," we insisted.

"I know that," said the young man, and went on.

"I'm from Anglian Water."

"Well, where do you suggest we pump the water to?" we asked.

"You can't pump it anywhere, you need a proper sludge pit, and filters."

"How do we get one of those?" we asked.

"Well, I don't know," he replied.

Now it was enough that a middle aged, suffering, wet and dirty and very disillusioned man and an equally, though not middle aged, suffering lady, were pushing wheelbarrows full of silt over long and hard distances, trying to create the best and only wild Swan hospital in the world, totally without help from anyone. What we did not need was to be pestered by a clip board carrying, pedantic schoolboy, telling us what we could and could not do. Adding to this unwelcomed interference, was the fact that during the last seven years, Eddie, Sheila, myself and Rina, on our own, cleared up oil slicks and other river pollution caused by the Anglian Water Authority, as they did not have the equipment, nor the knowhow. We cleared their rivers of dead birds and, above all, realised that Anglian Water were responsible for the deaths of thousands of waterbirds through injuries from Coarse fishing, which they promoted and lead poisoning, through failing to ban lead weights. Anglian Water Authority have a list of failures as long as your arm concerning pollution and wildlife.

This schoolboy from Anglian Water was telling us that we could not pump our dirty water, which was incidentally water from the farmer's fields that had drained into our pond, and also drained into our front drainage ditch – as is typical all over the British Isles. This, then, could not be accepted by the young man from Anglian Water. But it was all right and perfectly acceptable by him and his masters to drain raw sewerage into the rivers, of Great Yarmouth for example, with solid human faeces and sanitary towels, flowing in full view through the holidaymakers and their children at the Marina in that town! We had lost many Swans through Salmonella poisoning after eating this effluent at Great Yarmouth. We traced the outlet to a riverside Caravan Park, where Salmonella was indeed confirmed by Anglian Water and where one of the residents of the Park had contracted the disease. This sewerage, to this day, can still be seen, flowing into the water of the river Bure at Great Yarmouth. This spectacle is regarded, by some, to be compulsive Sunday viewing.

The schoolboy scientist from Anglian Water continued with his pedantic mutterings. We exploded.

"Bugger off!" we told him. He now consulted his clip board.

"It is my duty," he started.

"Bugger off!" we interrupted. He went on.

"Under paragraph so and so of laws relating to so and so, I order you –"

"Sod off," we said. He didn't.

Now it is a strange fact of life that, for some reason, aggressive or official people do not like to be photographed. Rina fetched the camera. The Anglian Water schoolboy saw the camera. Rina clicked the shutter. He fled.

When we had pumped the worst of the black water away, we prepared the new Swan pond for its initial filling, with fresh, clean water. We rushed out and purchased one hundred metres of bright, brand new, yellow hose and connected this to our bore pump outlet. With misty coloured pictures of Swans enjoying their new lake, in our minds' eyes and with trembling hands, we turned on the brass tap. We waited a split second for the gurgling, bubbling, effervescent, life giving water to cascade from the end of our new yellow hose. We still waited, and then after a second or two some indescribable liquid, of the viscosity of brown sauce and the smell of eight thousand decomposing Dinosaurs, dredged up from the bowels of the earth, fell leadlike to the ground, about five drops to be precise. We waited. It did not improve. It was liquid rust. We looked at each other in total disbelief. Rina started to cry. After all this – not another problem surely. We couldn't take any more. We turned off the tap, although this was unnecessary, and sloped off towards the house. We were more than disillusioned, we were totally defeated. As Rina started to make a cup of tea, that traditional British panacea for all known problems, I noticed her hands. Her fingers were blue with cold.

Belton Marsh, Norfolk, family, all oiled due to one of Anglian Water's pumps failing. August 1988.

Great Yarmouth, Norfolk.

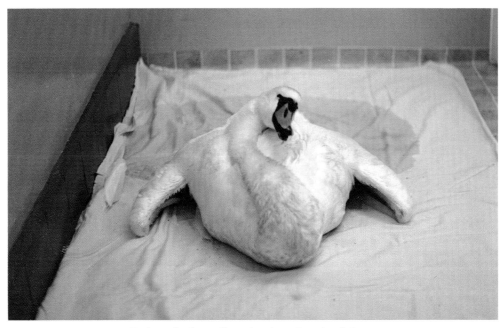

Dying of salmonella poisoning. Result of above.

All this, just because we all loved a bird.

The tea worked its age old magic and with the strength of the Swans behind us, urging us to carry on, we started to make enquiries to various companies within the field of water treatment. After speaking with several people that seemed to be scattered around the Norfolk countryside and failing to understand them, not being able to employ the services of a translator, we finally ended up with a young man from Norwich.

"You need filters," the aqua man said.

"How much are filters?" we enquired.

"I'll do you a quote," he said – and left.

We returned to the old cottage to tell Sheila and Eddie of the news. They were proceeding well with the unenviable task of packing and getting ready for the move to the new house. Eddie was still doing the rescues, Sheila the paper work. Eddie also had the Swans on the Costessey marsh to feed and maintain.

The quotation from the water treatment company came within a few days. It would cost us over £4,000 to get water to a condition good enough for our Swans. They had to have it. We instructed aqua man to proceed, leaving us to work out where the money was going to come from. Meanwhile Rina and I carried on fencing and building pens and digging more small therapy ponds, by hand, for the incoming injured Swans.

Within the next year we were settled in at Lathe Green and had built six ponds and also had a fully filtered swimming pool constructed for the free flying Swans, recovering from treatment. They could fly off whenever they felt fit enough. This new swimming pool we designed to have an exit ramp, that gave the Swans a clear, uninterrupted flight path that would take them up and over the old pond, to freedom. Fly away they did, only to return later, after a few laps at a hundred feet or so above the flat Norfolk farmland and then settle back with us and the other Swans. So they preferred this then, this makeshift paradise, to freedom. But where, and what, is freedom?

Freedom, we have been taught, is a state of mind, a satisfaction of the spirit. It is not a place. There are no places of freedom for the Mute Swans of the British Isles, in a practical sense. Sure you will still see flocks of Swans, in various places, but these places of freedom, to the casual observer anyway, are their interpretations of Swans that are free. This freedom has cost the Swans their independence, and independence is an ingredient of real freedom. They are in places where they are fed by humans so are dependent upon those humans. Apart from some areas we have seen in the Highlands of Scotland, Britain's Mute Swan, to guarantee survival, has had no choice but to become a semi-domesticated scrounger. Unlike the beautiful wild Bewick Swan from Russia, and the Whooper Swan from Greenland and Iceland who are still, thank God, relatively wild Swans. The exceptions being those Swans who frequent, during migration, the many wildfowl reservations. There they are fed by men, with wheelbarrows full of wheat, being attracted by other pinioned wild Swans and encouraged for people to see. These Swans will lose, with their dependence upon man, that invisible quality that is the essence of freedom.

All Swans graze – hundreds of them upon the marshes and winter wheat, all over the British Isles. We have only ever met one farmer that accepts, and indeed allows, grazing by Swans upon his land. In most cases the Swans are discouraged, so have no choice but to head for, and eat, the food offered by the wildfowl reservations. More of this later.

So our Swans, then, came home to Lathe Green and, sometimes, would bring friends with them. They were, of course, welcome, but with the Swans from Costessey now with us, space was becoming a continual problem. We had to speed up the removal of Swans from Costessey, owing to troubles with the neighbours and the still existent problems with the power cables that littered that area of Norfolk.

To ensure safety then for any incoming flying Swans at Lathe Green, we had to find three thousand pounds, to give the Eastern Electricity Board of Norwich, for burial of a power cable that stretched across the rear of our new swimming pool. This money was raised by our Swan Lady and one of our best fundraisers, Joan Walls of Pakefield. The fact that the Eastern Electricity Board charged the Swans three thousand pounds for this service, gives you some idea of the extent of their concern for the wildlife they destroy. Ironical, when you consider that the Swans in our care at Lathe Green, that we had brought from Costessey, were crippled by power cable collisions. Now we had to pay. So pay we did.

We had, within the last few years, made great advances with our treatments and diagnosis of Swan ailments and had learnt a great deal about the diseases of wild waterfowl. The Government's ban on the sale of certain sizes of lead weights did not make any noticeable difference, however, to the number of lead poisoned Swans we were treating, especially Swans unfortunate enough to swallow the larger leger weights, still lawful under the Government's new regulations. Nor indeed with the very small weights, known as "dust shot". These "legal" weights were still killing Swans, as also was the lead from cartridge shot. Our campaigns against the use of these cartridges carry on to this day. It is unbelievable, but true, that at the time of writing, the International President of The Worldwide Fund for Nature, still uses lead filled cartridges for his hobby of killing Pheasants.

These cartridges are also used for the popular sport of Clay Pigeon shooting and, indeed, we recently lost an entire flock of non breeding Swans from an area near us at South Walsham. Their local Clay Pigeon club had shot over an area abutting South Walsham Broad. The shot is everywhere, in the woods, on the edge of the Broad, the pathways are made of spent lead shot, its dykes and drains are full of the stuff. The only solution for this area would be a two foot thick layer of concrete over all of it. Waterbirds will be picking up this toxin for years, and have been.

The original pond after cleaning out. Lathe Green.

The £17,000 swimming pool. Lathe Green.

After our complaints to this particular Club, they at least moved their shoot elsewhere. By moving they admitted their guilt. There are hundreds of these clubs in the British Isles. Every bang you hear is three hundred and sixty pieces of lead in our environment. Clay Pigeon clubs, therefore, should not be given permission to shoot over, or adjacent to, waterways.

We discovered that nickel filled cartridges were available in England for shooters, but they still preferred to use the lead filled cartridge. One of their arguments being that with its higher density, lead shot gave a "cleaner" kill.

We have, under duress, watched a Pheasant shoot. Many of the poor birds were still struggling through long death throes, minutes after being peppered with lead shot. So with Ducks and more so with wild Geese. It is our opinion that, if it is impossible for Man to bridge the gap in evolutionary growth and cease, with the help of modern technology, to be the hunter provider, then the least he could do would, surely, be to kill cleanly. He should kill only the bird or animal he feels he has to kill and not leave, in his path, thousands of pieces of lead shot for other wildlife to ingest and slowly die, the long, painful death of lead poisoning.

It is a pity that the Duke of Edinburgh cannot, or will not, spearhead the campaign to use substitute shot. The many minions that make up the aristoc-racy, and the shooting set of England, would probably emulate their respected Royal fellow hunter. Thousands of innocent birds lives would be saved and the Duke of Edinburgh would slightly, but only slightly, start to justify his position as President of the Worldwide Fund for Nature.

We were, after the move to Lathe Green farmhouse, soon back into the swing of petitioning and campaigning. This was helped greatly by our acquisition of cameras and our close proximity to an excellent, cheap printer. We sent, with our Newsletters, thousands of campaign postcards, to the electricity boards throughout England and to the Duke of Edinburgh. This we still continue to do. Of course to date, we have never received a reply from the offices of Buckingham Palace. But we have, in our work for Swans, made absolutely certain that we will not have to go through the worry of trying to raise money for the purchase of new clothing, in which to accept our Knighthoods! This you can imagine, is a great relief.

We continued rescues, treatments, minor surgery, maintenance and the production of fundraising merchandise, unaided. Life was made easier for the Swans requiring X-rays, when a lady from Kent presented us with a brand new X-ray machine. It was a most welcome gift. School children from Essex raised money and with it bought the Swans a new outboard boat engine and surgical dressings, and a

Swans in our care, all suffering terminal sickness through the ingestion of clay pigeon shot. Recovered from South Walsham Broad, Norfolk.

kind supporter from Leicestershire raised enough money to buy a brand new inflatable boat for Eddie. We had used, already, six inflatable boats, which were now unsafe, and worn out seven assorted cars and vans. Our merchandise proved very popular, as all design, photography, drawings and artwork were executed by us. There are only four of us but within our pathetically small "family", we have our own individual talents. This has been a blessing to the Swans, saving them thousands of pounds from their pitifully low bank account. We have never had to pay outside contractors for any of the above work. This, of course, giving all our products and merchandise the valuable stamp of originality.

With our incredible work load, we would have to work up to eighteen hours a day, every day, to keep up. We were, of course, very tired but then one of those pieces of magic would come into our lives, like a ray of sunshine on an overcast day.

One of these pieces of magic came in the shape of a Bewick Swan. She had flown, as is usual in autumn, all the way from her native Russia, to spend the milder winter with us in England. Eddie brought her in from a local area that was covered in overhead power cables.

Bewick Swans are the most difficult to work on, owing to their wildness. They are very easily stressed. This poor little Cygnet had three compound fractures in her left wing, thanks to the power cable, and was bleeding profusely. Knowing that she could never fly again, we made our usual light aluminium surgical splint for her shattered wing. We stopped the bleeding, gave her an antibiotic injection and the minimum treatment, so handling was reduced. We decided to leave her alone, in a pen with other power cable amputees, to help ease her stress and to check her again, if of course she lived, in six weeks' time. She was very nervous of the other Swans, who were up to twice her size, so as was expected, took a few days before settling down. Some four days passed, in fact, before she was taught by the other Swans how to find the food bowl. It was obviously the first time, in this young Swan's life, that she had been apart from her parents. Bewicks fly from Russia in family groups and this was her first trip. We marked her operation date in the hospital record book and left her alone. She seemed to form a close friendship with our crippled Whooper Swan, he being the only other Swan we had with a yellow beak, just like that of her parents. We dreaded the day when we had to catch her again to remove her splint. We have always hated catching Swans, it makes us feel dirty and, it gives us an attitude of a predator to the Swans. That is why we always spoke to Swans and wildlife when capturing, predators do not speak. It always seemed to work. So much so, that when people saw Swans sitting in our car, or on our operating table, so still and well behaved, they asked if the Swan was under sedation. He was, our voices being the sedative.

The day before the removal of the splint was due, Rina found a piece of plaster and aluminium, on the ground in the amputee pen. Bewicks obviously had,

probably tucked under their wings, their own calendar, for our little Russian friend had, one day before it was due, removed her own splint! We were more than delighted. We put her with the flying Swans and she stayed with us for some considerable time. She preferred the company of old Whoopie and the Canada Geese and grew into a beautiful, pure white adult Bewick Swan. She never lost her wild spirit, and in fact became wilder as she became stronger. She would exercise her wings constantly, then one day was seen actually flying four foot above the ground. The slight kink still visible in her wing, but flying all the same. This exercise in "benign neglect" proving to be the best treatment for broken wings, in our experience, it definitely proved more successful than pinning.

Then, on one clear, bright late spring day, two years later, obeying a call as old as time and heard only by the creatures of the wild, Bewick left us.

We hope this tiny lady of freedom arrived home in Russia safely. We miss her very much. It was a pleasure knowing her. She was last seen at an altitude of some hundred feet, above the other Swans, flying very strongly, she had lapped the hospital once and headed in a northerly direction, known only by herself.

The isolation of Lathe Green was both a blessing and a curse. We were surrounded by shooters. The shooting was run by a man from a village close by who would have, years ago, carried the title of "The Squire". He looked as though he had slipped from the advertising pages of a shooting magazine. Flat check cap, check shirt, nondescript dark green tie, corduroy trousers, wax cotton jacket and green wellington boots. He had, as a constant companion, a Jack Russell terrier. The terrier we liked! He had that annoying way about him of not looking at you, eye ball to eye ball, when talking with you. The tit bits of conversation we were forced, at times of confrontation to indulge in, were conducted with eyes seemingly fixed upon an invisible object some two hundred miles away.

He had control over a fair amount of land and over a small copse to the right and opposite our farmhouse, It was in this copse that he bred his Pheasants for eventual "sport". This tiny domain was his kingdom and he would patrol the boundaries of his kingdom with all the authority of a redundant traffic warden. When, trying to instigate conversation with us, he would, using his obsequious tone, expound upon his theories and knowledge of wildlife, with all the verve and experience of a six and a half year old child, suffering a mental relapse! He and his friends, with their various pick-up trucks and Land Rovers, would arrive on Wednesday mornings and re-enact what sounded to us like the Battle of the Somme. The squire and his underlings were having their usual fun. The Swans inside our hospice, some trying to die peacefully and with dignity, were terrified. Their bag for the day would include anything that flew, hopped or ran, fur or feather. It also sadly included the Ducks that lived with our Swans on the ponds. When seeing

Bewick Cygnet, arrival at surgery.

Same Bewick flying home, now white and now free!

one of our Ducks looking lame or finding their carcass, we would X-ray the poor creature and see the tiny white dots upon the film, depicting the twelve bore shot.

The expenses of running the hospital, were exceedingly high. We would, when time allowed, try to top up the Swans' bank account with money from personal sources, selling pictures for example. My little book, *Marlon, the Story of a Swan*, gave the Swans a few thousand pounds and each member of the team and indeed part-time helpers Bert and Joyce Green, Jean and Kip Kirby and Sylvia from Peterborough, would not only contribute, but would pay for petrol for rescues out of their own pockets. None of them, or us, ever took a wage or expenses. We were delighted to find out that a very large, multi million pound organisation, the Norwich Union Insurance Company, would help us financially if we became a proper Registered Charity. The day came. We were attending the launch of Pamela Townsend's book on our work, at a well known department store in Norwich. It was after hours and the store had kindly allowed the use of their restaurant for the launch. We were asked to step into the middle of the crowd, to accept the cheque. This then was it! We knew that the people who were presenting the cheque were from the Norwich Union Insurance Company. Over the three metre distance to accept the cheque, I had already spent it in my technicolour imagination. I had bought two islands, the Atlantic ocean, eight million acres of grazing and three houses for individual Swan hospitals, a rescue helicopter and for myself, a cassette of Mahlers Fifth Symphony. I reached out to accept the cheque and with misty eyes, gazed with beautiful anticipation at the amount.

The Norwich Union Insurance Company had given the Swans of England, twenty five pounds!

PART II

RINA'S STORY

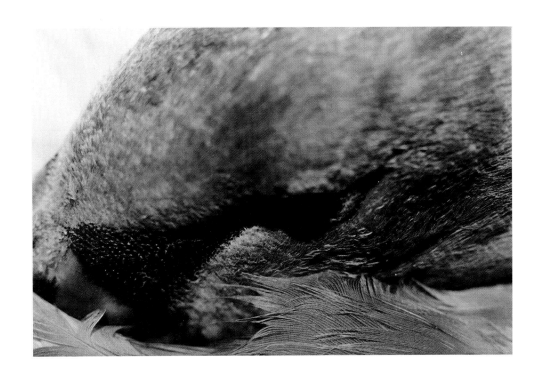

CHAPTER 6
First Meeting

As the car turned the corner into the lane, and on into the farm drive, my surprise turned into disbelief. Could this really be the world's only fulltime Swan Rescue centre? A tiny, dilapidated, farm worker's cottage with crumbling, abandoned, outhouses and barns, of a farm long ago forgotten when big machinery, sprays and technology changed the face of our countryside. Farm workers were replaced by combine harvesters. Small farms were now replaced by agrifactories. Hedgerows were torn down and pretty patchwork fields, of the picture postcard England, were to become prairies of disinterest.

Then I saw the Swans, to the front, rear and side of the old cottage. Their confines were very limited but they seemed completely at peace, going about their business, quite unaware of the sound of the car as it drew up. Some were pecking at the aggregate or small patches of grass. Others had their beaks submerged in large bowls full of water and wheat. Many were busy preening their plumage into some sort of order, though the many obvious injuries and their illhealth made this an arduous task. The tiny manmade concrete or plastic ponds, seemed to be overflowing with Swans. Only the few Canada, or Greylag geese and ducks, breaking the snow white covering of the water. Some Swans were simply sleeping, heads tucked under a wing, but always alert, peaking a glance my way, in case a predator may be around. I was very flattered when they looked at me and went straight back to sleep, after working out I was of no threat to them. All was peaceful, and a strange quiet seemed to hang over this tiny haven as I opened the gate into the front garden, beneath the branches of the big copper beech tree.

So this was my first meeting with the big white winged ones. A one time friend took me to the cottage, after telling me the Bakers were in need of help. I stayed for a weekend. Several more weekend visits, all the way from London, some hundred or so miles away, prompted me to move to Norfolk and give more time to the Swans. I found it difficult to believe that help was not flocking in from authorities or from those in large established animal welfare groups. Swans were coming in from everywhere in England, at an alarming rate, suffering from lead poisoning, fishing tackle injuries, power cable collisions, pollution, vandalism, and road traffic accidents. My part time help not being sufficient, I made the decision and Ernie, my dog, and I set out to find somewhere to live in Norfolk, near to the Swans. A promise made to an old Indian, when I was living in America some years ago, helped bring my decision to fruition. Working with the Indians in their struggles against genocide was not so different, I thought, to the struggles of these Swans.

Out of time, out of place, in this modern materialistic world we have created. Struggling for survival, against all odds, simply trying to exist. That old Indian made me promise that I would never stop helping his people. I had to leave that country but now I would fulfil that promise made in California. The Swans are his people, they are our people, they simply have no voice, unlike the indigenous people of America, so they needed my help all the more. It was a strange link, a mysterious path that led me to Len Baker and his Swans, for he too had met these Native Americans some years earlier. Do we really think we are masters of our own destiny? I think not. The Swans chose me – not I them.

So my career as a draughtswoman in London had come to a close, for a time at least, or so I thought. I was about to embark upon a long journey that would take me to the depths of despair in suffering with a creature who embraces the spirits of us all, if only we allow ourselves to see and feel it. Yet in between that suffering, these mystical birds give you glimpses of beauty and magic that give you an inner strength and so help you carry on. For without the Swans I would now be lost.

I arrived at the small bungalow I had managed to find to rent with Ernie, the dog, beside me, feeling very afraid of the step I had taken. I had given up my job, and a regular wage, for a Swan who could not pay me in money but whose reward proved far greater. The bungalow was only a mile from the newly purchased sanctuary that Len and Sheila had found. Their back garden, where I had first met them and the Swans, was full to overflowing with injured Swans, so the new fifteen acre marsh sanctuary was essential. During my weekends to Norfolk I had been involved in building new pens on this marsh, to house the pairs of Swans who had permanent wing injuries, cruel legacies from power cable collisions, and the many similar non breeding flock of Swans who were in desperate need of more water to swim and bathe. A new hospital facility was planned for the sanctuary that would house the terminally sick Swans, suffering from lead poisoning, Botulism or Aspergillosis. It was the first hospital of its kind, so there were no ideas to be gleaned from anywhere else, but living with Swans in a cottage, and a back garden full of them, you get to know a bit about them and their needs. Apart from a few part-time helpers, Len and Sheila had no one full time, until now. Shortly after my move to Norfolk, Eddie Bush, who had been helping part time, also gave up his full-time occupation to devote himself fully to the Swans. He is with us to this day. Without him and his undying strength, we – Len, Sheila and I – would probably not be alive today. It was Eddie that took over most of the Swans rescue side of our service, in the last few years, when Len became physically too ill to continue. That story will unfold later. The story I have to tell starts in October 1982 when my life became one with the Swans, as I lived and died with them, treating them where possible, to see them fly away sometimes but then to see them return either dead or injured.

My days soon became full with hard physical work, and all thoughts of a drawing board and set squares vanished. There were therapy ponds to pump out and clean, food bowls to fill, wound dressings to change and new bedding to make in the crowded kitchen of Len and Sheila's cottage, outside pen enclosures to hose clean of Swans' faeces and then in the afternoon I would work on the new sanctuary at Costessey. Evenings, after a rushed dinner, if we were not interrupted with rescue calls, consisted usually of treatments. In those days we were still using several chemicals, by injection, in a vain attempt at treating lead poisoned Swans. It was early days, before we realised the obvious. How can you hope to cure lead poisoning if pieces of lead are still in the Swan's gizzard, and toxins already affecting his blood, organs and tissues. You can temporarily alleviate the symptoms but never eliminate the cause, and so death always eventually occurred. But this was all we had, there was no one to ask for help and, apart from a young veterinary surgeon in Windsor, we at Swan Rescue were the pioneer task masters at treating Swans. So we were learning by trial and error, perhaps, and at the cost of Swans lives and their terrible suffering. The Government's conservation watchdog, the Nature Conservancy Council, had not seen fit yet to ban lead fishing weights, though themselves had estimated some four thousand Swans were dying every year from the effect of ingested lead fishermen's weights.

The Costessey sanctuary was taking shape and filling rapidly with Swans. We managed to afford two secondhand mobile trailer units, which we converted into a surgery and hospital, this being a vain attempt to clear the cottage kitchen. Most times, however, both the cottage and the new hospital were full of Swans, as more and more people throughout England, and the rest of Europe, heard of our twenty-four hour Swan Rescue Service. At Costessey we built five large pens with ponds to house our resident pairs and, when the first dyke pens filled with recuperating Swans, we had a small lake dug out by a contractor. We had plans to establish this and make it into as natural a lake as a Swan would hope to find, but as we put the first Swans in far sooner than we intended, the Swans uprooted our newly planted reeds and water plants. We were exhausted and disappointed at our wasted efforts at planting aqua vegetation, but the Swans were delighted with their new lake.

My bungalow was now too far away, the travelling cutting down my precious working day, there was so little time to complete all the necessary tasks. The sanctuary needed constant maintenance work. There were new pen enclosures to build, old ones to mend and more ponds to clean. Eddie was needed close at hand, so we decided to rent a little cottage on the edge of the sanctuary when it became vacant. Eddie, Ernie the dog and I moved in, with our few possessions and the tiny cottage, very cold and very damp, became a base during those dark days of endless, depressing, backbreaking work. We were doing between ten and twenty Swan rescues a day, at that time, travelling all over the British Isles, wherever a Swan needed our help. Eddie and I formed one rescue team, Sheila and Len the other, until arthritis limited Sheila's activity. Len's time with the Swans was also becoming limited, as he was trying to find ways to pay the enormous bills of running the service. Our new rented cottage, by the sanctuary, was always full of part-time helpers who never stayed for long. It was hard work but, most of all, it is not easy when you see animals die, day after day. Most helpers left after hearing or seeing their first Swan death.

In 1983 I promised a certain Swan, a special Swan, I would never leave him and his friends and I haven't to this day, years later, and I never will. The following is the story of this special Swan and those friends.

CHAPTER 7
Woody's Story

The rescue call came from that black spot for Swans, Epping Forest in London. This area has within it several areas of water, used extensively for coarse fishing by the local inhabitants. We have been called, by members of the public who enjoy the many waterbirds on these lakes, to rescue Swans here, repeatedly. The problems to the waterbirds are caused by heavy fishing and complete lack of management on behalf of the local Council and its staff. Discarded fishing tackle can be found all round the water's edge and with this, of course, will be found the lethal lead weights. Hence every rescue call we have had to this area resulted in a Swan either injured by fishing tackle or suffering from lead poisoning.

The lady who called us this time said the young Swan, a nearly full grown Cygnet, seemed lethargic, was not eating and had separated from the other Swans and gone to a quiet backwater. We typically noted down all the details and, only too well, recognised all the symptoms described to be those of lead poisoning. As the Cygnet was not eating, we knew it was going to be a difficult rescue, this meant we would need our inflatable rescue boat and our specially designed catching equipment. These are the rescues we dread, as they mean chasing a Swan, something that is abhorrent to us. Ultimately, when an angler hurts a waterbird, simply by his careless attitude of leaving behind him discarded tackle, it is

us who end up frightening the Swan by the chase. To a wild creature, especially a bird, being touched by a human is very stressful, this is natural as he supposes us to be a predator out for the kill. The chase obviously adds to these feelings of fear.

When a Swan can still eat, we simply feed him to us and take him by surprise.

When we arrived at Woodford, in the Epping Forest, Eddie, Len and I started our usual search for the Swan. We only had about two hours of light left, being late summer, the days were shortening. The area the lady caller had described was overgrown, with trees and shrubs, and had small muddy pathways, well trodden by people using the forest for recreation. The three of us separated to encompass the whole pond area and started the search for our Cygnet, by foot. We were told there was a small stream leading off the pond, so we headed off in its direction. As I walked along, small shapes on the ground, the size of large pebbles appeared all along the pathway. Then they started moving. I wasn't wearing my glasses, as I never do when I am about to be involved in a Swan rescue, for fear of having them knocked off by the large wings, when he flaps on catching. The most oft quoted warning is that a Swan can break your arm with a strike from the wing, but I daren't let him break my spectacles! The small pebble shapes were now hopping about everywhere and Eddie and Len called out to say that they too were

surrounded by frogs! At least this water was good for them.

It took about thirty minutes to locate the Cygnet, who was drifting about the mouth of the stream, at the back of the pond, amongst the undergrowth. Typical actions of a sick Swan. The look of the Cygnet was all too familiar. The informant was right to have called us. The Cygnet's neck had that typical "kink" at the base, was fluffy and he had no interest in the bread that we threw him. We would have to go back to the ambulance and launch the inflatable boat.

The three of us, in the inflatable, approached him with stealth, the outboard motor just ticking over. But this young Swan knew, as they always do, just what we were up to. He let us get quite close, then took off and flew very low past us through a gap between us and the bank. So the awful chase began. The chase is the part we hated most. You wonder whether it would be kinder just to leave them to die where they are, on their water. We have questioned ourselves on this point, time and time again. We will never know the answer. Only the Swan knows that, in the end. But we have, at least, learned when to stop the chase. A Swan will tell you that.

The Swans have taught us the precious gift of communication, without the use of words. I can now tell what a Swan is suffering from, simply by looking at him. Whether he has lead poisoning, an infection, Botulism or Aspergillosis. These abilities have been taught to us by the Swans. It has been an invaluable gift, and has helped us in saving many lives. Speed of treatment is, of course, the essence to recovery in many cases.

This Cygnet kept us on the chase for nearly an hour, but finally, after several failed attempts at cornering him, Eddie managed to catch him with his Swan hook, from the boat. We were all tired, very wet and stressed, but none of us suffering as badly as the Cygnet, who had barely enough strength left to fight. However, as on so many occasions, his instinct for survival had given the little chap hidden strength.

Now he was in my arms and immediately he was calmed by the warmth of my body, the pulse of my heartbeat. Once you hold a Swan close to you he seems to know you mean no harm and he will cling to you, coiling his long graceful neck around yours, making you both feel at peace. As I gently wrapped the towel about him, to contain his wings, in case he should suddenly flap, I felt his thin body. The wasting effects induced by lead poisoning. When post mortem reports state that death was due to starvation it is often, nearly always, lead poisoning that brings this result. Lead poisoning causes complete paralysis of muscles, including those of their digestive system. This Cygnet weighed, though nearly fully grown, only about ten pounds, when he should have weighed at least twice that.

We drove home to Norfolk, feeling all our usual emotions at times like this. Anger is always top of the list. Somewhere out there, at home, or out for the evening, probably feeling warm and comfortable, is the fisherman who caused this. His discarded tackle brought this creature of beauty and freedom to this terrible condition, at so young an age. He was less than one year old. This thought welled up in us every time we rescued a Swan with fishing tackle entangling him or dying from lead poisoning. This could be up to fifteen Swans, every day, seven days a week, and these were only the ones we knew about. Every fisherman we have ever met has told us it was never his fault.

"I'm careful with my tackle," they say.

I'd like to know who else, then, uses fishing line, hooks and lead weights?

I did not know at this time the importance of this young Swan, who we later named Woody, being from Woodford. How he would be the "special" Swan, that Len told me, and tried to warn me, would appear one day. Who would make me discard all thoughts of ever being "normal" again.

A Swan that stood out from all the others I would rescue and treat, who would make me give up all human desires, needs and wants and give my whole being, and my very soul, willingly, to him and his kind. Len said this had happened to him, long ago. His Swan was called Marlon.

Mine, then, was to be Woody, but I didn't know this until a few weeks later. He just kept looking at me, with that strange, half turn of the head only he had. Always friendly, but always aloof. Always beckoning me, but never allowing me to get too close. Watching, studying, seeping slowly into my spirit. Then he would "parp", that strange in between voice, the noise that a young Swan makes when his voice is changing, from a squeak to a full grown healthy "grunt". That sound brought me back to reality and I would go about my business of feeding the other three hundred or so Swans we had at this time. But I could always see Woody now, watching me, wherever I was, no matter how far away, whatever I was doing. Guilt would overcome me if I was doing anything not directly to do with Swans. Even having a much needed bath. So this is what Woody was up to. Clever Swan! We did our usual X-ray of Woody, as we do with all incoming Swans, and it was revealed, as expected, split shot lead fishermen's weights, in his gizzard. He was in a poor way and we had no hopes for his survival. We treated him in the usual way, in those days, with an injection of EDTA, which seemed to help their discomfort but was always questionable as to whether it was the injection or the tummy full of Complan that actually helped. He seemed to like this creamy liquid very much and was always asking for more.

We kept him for a few days in the garden, at the cottage, before I took him to our sanctuary, where nearly all the Swans now were. Only new patients were kept at the old cottage at Sparham, before they were moved to our long term hospice, where I was taking charge of all treatments, therapy and day to day care of the Swans. Eddie helped with the feeding, but maintenance took most of his time. We were also called out, several times a day, for rescues. My day started with the six a.m. feed and check on all

Swans at the sanctuary, a snatched coffee, then the feeding of the three hundred or so Swans. This was incredibly hard and difficult work. A wheelbarrow loaded with up to sixty kilograms of wheat, pushed for great distances, through rutted, slippery, black peat, many times a day. The loaded barrow continually burying itself, up to its axle.

This was difficult enough, but we had the added problem of having no running water at all. This made the operation of the hospital unit a dreadful chore. Water was not only needed for the hygiene demanded by the hospital, but to add to the food bowls. Waterbirds needing wet food. The only way to get water to the hospital unit was to carry two, five gallon, plastic containers, one in each hand, the four hundred odd metres from the river, the only source of water. This journey, over the rutted wheelbarrow tracks, was undertaken several times each day. It was exhausting work but I lost weight and developed biceps that would shame a Sydney lifesaver!

Woody was eating his soft food diet, of Vitalin dog cereal in water, very well now. He still slept a lot, in his little hospital pen, with its tiny paving slab pond but seemed, to us, to be responding to his treatment. After my morning feeding regime, I would do my injection treatments for the lead poisoned Swans. There were usually around fifteen to twenty in the unit, receiving treatments, every day. Woody took his place with them for the usual ten day course. He couldn't walk far but was gaining in strength, so I put him with a group of other Swans, who were in various stages of recuperation.

One morning, when I was doing my normal check, he seemed very quiet. I had only been with the Swans for about one year, at this time, the end of 1983, but I was learning to know them rapidly, spending every minute of my time with them, left alone to make the decisions on when and who to treat, and with what. Sheila was looking after the

new arrivals at Sparham, but mainly taking care of the increasing office work, made greater by the increasing readership of our twice yearly Newsletter. Len was busy with rescue work, as Eddie and I could not manage all the rescues at the rate they were coming in. Len was also receiving new patients at the cottage but now was obviously feeling the effects of the last five or so years, working alone. Unbeknown to Eddie and I, he was also working from midnight to four a.m. on his drawing board, designing new hulls for the French hire boat industry. The money earned from this work helping to keep the rescue service afloat. Donations received through the post, from our delightful supporters, just not being sufficient to pay the frightening bills.

Meanwhile, I watched Woody several times during the day and became increasingly worried by his obvious deterioration. I decided to take him back to Sparham for Len's opinion, fearing the worst. He managed a bowl of Complan, so we put him in the front garden for the night. The next day I was busy feeding the other Swans before going to the sanctuary, as Sheila's arthritis was becoming worse, making feeding difficult, when a shout came from Len, inside the cottage. Woody had found the front door open and made his own way into the kitchen, where a bowl of Complan was on the floor. He had helped himself to it and was looking around, with the sticky liquid dripping from his beak and down onto his neck. So his time was not up yet and I had learnt a bit more about Swans. After a few days at the cottage I took him back to the sanctuary and, after gaining more strength, I was able to put him in the dyke pen, with the fitter, mainly disabled, power cable Swans. Here he remained for several months and I continued to learn much from this magical little Swan.

His end came finally, not from lead poisoning, but something far more sinister. Woody's story will unfold later.

Living and working with Swans has enabled us to witness many instances, of what we call "Swan magic". Things that we, as rational, reasoning human beings, cannot explain, or hope to ever understand.

However, one particular example of this, I remember most vividly, was not with a Swan, but a Canada goose. She had been with us a long time. She had been living at the cottage at Sparham for two years, before being brought to the sanctuary and being placed upon our Swan lake. Suffering from lead poisoning, caused by the ingestion of twelve bore cartridge shot, she had always been very sick but had survived, somehow, for a long time, through our intensive feeding programme. The lead within her system had, however, caused muscle and nerve malfunction and given her a strange, staggering gait, when walking. She would walk backwards several steps but when attempting to move forward, would often topple. These symptoms eased gradually, enabling her to join our Swans.

Many wild flocks of geese used to fly in and out of the lake, scrounging the Swans food and flying off, without so much as a thankyou. We thought our Canada goose would be happy to be amongst her own kind again, and so she was, as she lived on the lake for another six months or so. It was hard at times to pick her out from the wild ones but she always stayed behind when they left, to seek freedom.

A magical thing happened one day when Len was making one of his frequent visits to the sanctuary, and we did our slow walk around the marsh, looking at the Swans. He liked to do this, as not only was he able to help check over the resident Swans but he may catch a glimpse of a flying visitor. This always amazed us, as our marsh ran alongside the River Wensum. For some reason the Swans ignored the river, with its relatively clean water and lush reed growth, to land in amongst our disabled, odd ball, group of Swans, with either wings, feet or eyes missing, or neck oddly kinked by blows from vandals. We always felt these visits by the wild ones to be a great honour, and welcomed them especially the two Barnacle geese, who came from who knows where, and stayed for over a year. Until one day the adjoining land owner saw fit to shoot one of them from the sky whilst he was flying low over the lake. His mate stayed for a while but eventually left us too.

As we reached the front of the lake, all the Swans started to call out. It was their alarm call, the sort of call a parent Swan cries if there is danger close by, threatening their offspring. We wondered what could be wrong, expecting to find a dead Swan in the lake. They had let me know this way before. We walked around the lake, until we saw a Swan that seemed to be leading us to where a small group had gathered. We still could not see anything out of place, until the same Swan swam fast, from the bank near to where we were standing, then across the lake toward one of the two islands. He then got out onto the island and stood calling with the group. They were surrounding the Canada goose. She was fighting for life, her head kept falling into the water but she was obviously far too weak to hold it up any more. We were powerless to help, but there was nothing we could do anyway. She had lived nearly three years with us, an amazing thing in itself, considering the state she was in. Now her time had come. So we watched, knowing that the next time her head fell into the water, it would be the end. As her head fell and we were saying goodbye, she suddenly did the impossible. As if driven by some invisible force, she started swimming directly toward me. The Swans now swimming in a line, astern, followed her, seemingly pushing her forward. She swam to the bank, toward my feet, I bent down and cupped my hands upon the surface of the water. Her wretched little sodden body was now lying in my hands. I lifted her from the water. The Swans, seeing she was now safe, turned away and swam from the scene. Len and I were speechless at what we had just witnessed. I held her close and life seeped from her beautiful, now not so wild, body. We will never understand these creatures fully, but every so often they show you a tiny piece of pure magic.

CHAPTER 8
Greenland Docks, London

There have been many frightening times when rescuing Swans. Not fear of a Swan – I have never felt fear of an animal. This is not always a particularly wise thing and has, in fact, ended up with me the worse off. Like the time I was so enraptured with a young farm horse, standing with its mother, and was so busy feeling the velvet softness of its brand new muzzle, he decided to test out his equally new teeth on my arm!

Rescuing Swans can, in itself, place you into very dangerous situations, especially, when like us all at Swan Resue, you are unable to swim.

Inevitably catching Swans leads you to water, and enormous risks have to be taken when battling with such a huge bird. Somehow, all reason vanishes when you see an animal in trouble and, after all the risks are taken and you slump back into the seat of the car, wet, cold and very uncomfortable, with nervous and physical exhaustion but with your Swan safely behind you, you suddenly realise what you have just done. You laugh, and agree with each other that you have committed an act of total insanity, then drive on to the next Swan that needs your help.

My most frightening moment was during the rescue of a whole family of Swans, stranded in the Greenland Docks of East London. The pair of Swans had lived here for many years and produced many broods of Cygnets, none of whom, sad to say, had survived. This was due to the polluted, oily water and total lack of any aqua vegetation, essential for the healthy growth of a young waterbird. The dock workers, big, tough, down to earth men, loved these Swans. They fed them every day – but they went to even far greater lengths, for their own white pieces of perfection, in a grubby, hard, world. They had, in their spare time, built a large floating raft with a small hut upon it, for the Swans in cold weather, and then each man, every day, had brought a bucket of earth from their homes and thrown it onto the raft. The seeds within this soil had flourished, and the growth of vegetation upon this tiny island was the only greenery the Swans had, in this cold, grey, concrete, man-made landscape, all around them. The Swans knew they were wanted here though, so had chosen it for their home and stayed, year after year. The streetwise London dockies watched over their charges with pride. Every year these Swans built their makeshift nest upon their island. The raft being secured to the main dock, by ties, from each corner, to iron rings embedded in the concrete wall.

Then dawned the age of micro-chip technology. These men of hard, honest toil, were being pushed out. One by one the dockyards were being closed.

Men were put out of work and families, the "real people" of London, were being moved on, to be rehoused in vast housing estates, featureless, meaningless, workless homes, for the no longer needed, in the new towns of the home counties. The docks were being redeveloped for the new people of London – the "yuppies". Warehouses were torn down, some converted into trendy houses and flats, and the docks themselves were turned into playgrounds for the rich, new residents. Yachts were now filling them, and this meant clearing out the aeons of debris that had lain dormant beneath the water, for generations. The Swans island just had to go – so did the Swans. There would be no room for them in this new world of pleasure craft, jet bikes, speedboats and water skiers. The dock workers called us and pleaded with us to take their Swans away to a safer place. They loved them that much. Loving is so often letting go. The men would soon be gone too.

When we arrived at Greenland Docks the water was covered with a film of oil, from the disturbance of the clearance programme, removing the many years' accumulation of dumped machinery. We had been told the family of Swans had fled in panic, ironically this year four Cygnets had survived – they were still only half fledged. They had escaped into a smaller dock that had no places for them to get out of the water – this being essential for preening their plumage to keep them waterproof. Without this important, two hourly, preening session, the water-proof quality of their plumage would be lost and drowning would be inevitable. The Cygnets were still covered in their brown-grey down, so it was a matter of speed being the essence. Hence our next reckless moves. The dockies greeted us, showed us to the Swans, and said there was no way that they could get to them. The Swans had got through two small gaps in the dock wall, where the water poured through as the tide ebbed and flowed. Between these was a small sluice, full of bits of wood and other debris. The tide was out and the Swans were deep in the dock, some fifty feet below us. There were bits of polystyrene floating by the edge and the Cygnets tried desperately to clamber upon them, feeling the weight of the water on their down, and knowing by instinct, they must preen to survive. The drop to the water was too far for us to launch our inflatable boat, so we had to just watch and hope that the tide would come in fast. After about an hour the water had risen sufficiently for us, we felt, to attempt a launch. The Swans were swimming round and round, unable to get back out through the gaps they had entered, which could only be reached when the water was high. We got our long ropes from the car, took the boat from the roof rack, tied the ropes to it and lowered the boat down the side of the dock wall to the surface of the water. It was now about thirty feet down, the tide was coming in but we could not wait any longer, as the Cygnets were dangerously waterlogged. The dockies stood back and watched, telling us they, "wouldn't go down there!"

"There's bodies darn there mate," one said.

"Fell darn there on 'is fork lift truck, cars an' all, darn there. Yer bleedin' mad to try it but God bless yer and good luck!"

The dockie held onto the ropes to the boat as we gingerly descended the slippery, narrow, iron steps of the dock wall ladder to the water. It seemed a very dark, cold place and the walls and the lock gates seemed very high, as we sat in our small inflatable. The dockies then lowered our outboard engine on a rope to us. We fitted it to the boat and started up. The family of Swans were watching us from the other side of the dock all the time. We proceeded toward them, slowly, trying not to panic them. They swam away from us, the parents protecting their babies from this big, grey, predator, coming at them. We followed them round and round the dock, the Cob Swan, now and then, taking short flights across the water. Although we were unaware of it, the water was still rising and had reached the level of the gap to the sluice. The adult Swans slipped in, with the Cygnets squeaking after them. We felt this might be a good place to catch them, so worked out a hasty plan. I stepped from the boat, onto the ledge of the gap, where the Swans had entered, so I could slip through into the sluice with them. Len would stay in the boat and block their exit. I would try and catch the Swans, on my own. We had not worked out, though, what I would do with the Swans when I had caught them. We were too anxious and worried about the state of the Cygnets, for slow, sensible thought.

I stepped onto some wooden pallets, dry at this time, in the sluice with the Swans. I decided, if I caught the Cygnets first, I could hand them up to the dockie, watching from above the sluice. He would not be afraid of handling one of these small, pathetic, little bundles, I thought. This was not our usual practice, it being far better to catch the Cob first, as he will obviously attack if you touch his babies, but this was not a typical situation. All Len could do was sit and watch, as I floundered on the unstable, wooden flotsam, lunging at the Swans. I caught one of the Cygnets and passed it to the dockie, delighted. I told him to put it in the back of our car. I grabbed another Cygnet and passed it to him when he returned, from what I thought was our car. I had a chance now to catch the Pen. Stumbling, shaking and trying hard not to listen to the jeers and snide comments of two youths, watching my desperate attempts to catch six Swans all on my own, because there was not a man amongst them who would dare to put himself in the position that I was. I caught her and, relieved, passed her up to the only helper we had, the dockie, who was at least brave enough to carry a Swan. Not many men are.

The sluice I climbed into with the Swans.

Pen and waterlogged Cygnets in dock.

Len was continuing to block the exit gap, as the Cob tried to get through it. Then I started to feel my bits of wood move beneath me. They had been lying on the bottom of the sluice, while the tide was out, with just a little water around them. Although the tide had been coming in all the while, I had not realised the speed it would rush through into the sluice, when it reached the height of the gap – I was trapped in a space of some twenty foot by ten foot only. The water suddenly poured in through the gap and my wood and bits of debris were now floating, with me teetering, terrified, on top of it. The youths above me now laughed and jeered even louder. I asked for help. None came. I grabbed one more Cygnet and somehow managed to grab at a rope, hanging from the side of the sluice. The Cob and the remaining Cygnet were now swimming free, and they managed to get through a gap into the cut that led out into the open water.

Len made his way, as fast as he could, in the boat to the steps, to come to my aid. I saw him standing at the top of the sluice, as I clung to my Cygnet, desperately now, trying to keep afloat on my piece of wood. The water was still pouring in as I started to clamber up the side of the sluice, my knees shaking with fear. I made it to the top and saw my two young tormentors fishing, on the side of the dock, after having their fun at my expense.

I stood at the top, with Len, the Cygnet still in my arms, my legs and feet soaked. The dockie had been holding on to the female Swan, which he now handed to Len. I looked down into the sluice from where I had just climbed. It was now nearly full of water and I briefly thought that I had a narrow

escape, before asking the dockie if the two Cygnets I had passed up were all right in the back of the car.

"Oh yeah," he said. "They're down there, in the cut!"

Len and I looked at each other with horror. The dockie's East End accent made car and cut sound the same and, suspecting the latter to be the most likely, never having seen Swans in the back of a car, he had put them in the cut. (Cut in Cockney, meaning canal.)

There was no time to get angry or upset, he had been trying to help, anyway. We hastily wrapped the Pen Swan and put her safely in the back of our car and went back for the boat. We launched it into the cut, between the small dock and the family's "home" dock and soon had the first two Cygnets, rescued a second time, wrapped up and with their mum in the back of the car. Now we had to go back and find the Cob and the fourth Cygnet. Somebody shouted and pointed, so we guessed it must be the Swans. They had gone round to a gravel beach area, scattered with rocks and broken concrete. We rushed round in the boat, hoping to catch them on the land. I said I would go for the Cygnet, as I can run faster than Len, while he would try for the Cob, who was closer. The trick used in situations like this, is to keep yourself between the Swan and the water. This is very tricky, as you cannot outrun a Swan. We both went about our task, without uttering, both trying to outwit our chosen Swan. I managed to grab my Cygnet, just as he started to dart back to the water, when I heard a yell from Len. I looked around to see him, sprawled out on the beach, with the Cob in his arms, but something seemed to be wrong. The Swan was

flapping and Len did not seem to be able to move. When I reached them both I saw why. On lunging for his Swan he had tripped on a long, tangled length of heavy, sea fishing line. It was caught all around his leg so he was unable to move. But he had the Swan. I tucked the Swan's huge wings in safely into Len's arms and disentangled Len's legs from the wretched, discarded, fishing line. At last we had the whole family. It had been a terrible ordeal.

After a cup of tea, kindly provided from the flask of some onlookers, we loaded the boat on the car and set off, with our family of Swans, now safely together, in the back of the car. They were quite content now they were all together again and, as all Swans do, started to enjoy their ride in the car.

We had arranged to take them to the Hare Krishna group, at their base in Letchmore Heath, Hertfordshire, bought for them by George Harrison of the Beatles. They had written to us, saying they would love a pair of Swans for the lake in their grounds. Somewhat naively we trusted them, completely, as Swans were believed by them to be the embodiment of their spirit. We forgot our usual rule and did not check the lake first, as we always did when rehousing Swans upon private lakes.

When we arrived the Krishnas were having some kind of religious feast, and greeted us and the Swans warmly. It came, therefore as a great shock when one of the robed women told us that they were dredging the lake, in a month's time. We were very angry, and made them promise they would not do this. They only agreed to abandon their plans when they understood we would take the Swans away, if they dredged the lake. We did not know how we were going to do this, as we had already released the Swans onto their lake, and it would mean rescuing them all over again! We still had not dried out from our ordeal at the Greenland Docks.

Tempers calmed, we drove away, after checking the Swans, who seemed happy exploring their new home. It was not until three months had passed, when we received a phone call from a Veterinary surgeon in Watford, that we found out the fate of the family. Apparently the Cob had escaped, three of the Cygnets were dead, the Pen was still on the lake, as far as they knew, but they had the fourth Cygnet in care. It had been with them for several weeks, in a very poor way. We drove down to Watford to collect the Cygnet. She had not grown at all, was very thin and had a swollen, infected leg. She lived only a few more days in our care. We do not know the reasons for the tragic end to this family, but we have had several bad experiences when we have tried to house Swans on private lakes. Eventually we stopped this altogether. Many people want Swans simply to adorn their lakes. They did not realise they would need caring for, and time, and money spent on food. A Swan knows when he is loved and when he is not. Swans only settle if the place is right. Sometimes the places chosen by the Swans, are those places humans would consider most unlikely. The prime evolutionary consideration for wild birds, obviously, is that of ample food suplies. These places can be the worst waterways you can imagine. The wild places have disappeared, Swans now live where they are fed by humans.

CHAPTER 9
Sanctuary. Costessey, Norfolk

Many Swans came and went through my hospital unit, on the sanctuary, at Costessey. I got to know them all, intimately. Treating them all alone, dressing their wounds, cleaning their pens and, where necessary, giving orthopaedic therapy. We often had Swans with internal injuries, including brain damage, and these had to be taught, in many cases, to walk again. They may have fallen hard, after hitting a power cable, or, as in the case of one Swan we called King Kenneth, from Gloucestershire, may have received a blow to the head. So often these injuries are received by being hit with the oar of a boat, by some idiot wanting the waterway, all to himself.

This Cob Swan must have been magnificent, before this tragedy occurred, when he was fit and on his water. He was immensely strong, very large and very heavy. His brain damage had left him completely unable to walk. When he attempted to, he just stumbled and fell at first. I decided to try and help him, in his obviously determined attempts to be a Swan again. He did not take too kindly to being touched, it being beneath his dignity. He had obviously been an old warrior, on the river, no doubt having a mate somewhere and a territory of their own. He would have fought many battles with other Swans, first to gain, then to retain, this territory. So being fussed over, by a mere eight stone female, was very demeaning to his pride.

However, I persevered and managed, after several, one hour sessions, walking him up and down, taking the full weight of his body, to teach him to take several steps before eventually falling again. After one of these sessions, I was sitting down eating my sandwich as I sat with the Swans, when King Kenneth staggered to his feet and charged forward, fell and charged forward, again, all the time towards the dyke pen. I was amazed and proud of his, and my, achievement.

He must be dying to have a good bath, I thought. I had not been able to put him near water because he would have drowned, being unable to right himself, when he fell on his side. All coordination goes, with brain damage, and they are left with partial use of muscles only. The time had come to give him a try in the water. Better now he should die clean, where he wants to be, than away from his beloved water. So I carried him for the last few yards, a feat in itself, as he pushed and struggled so hard, when picked up. I put him in the water with the other Swans. He darted round, tipped, righted himself, just, round again, his head dipped under the refreshing cool water, flapping his wings, in an attempt at a bath and, all in all, had a thoroughly good time.

He carried on like this for about half an hour, before finally he staggered and stumbled up the wooden ramp, to the top of the bank. He had done it! All on his own. Truly a warrior. Now I must leave him. I had done all the good I could for him. He would never fully recover but he was a Swan again.

Apart from the many individual needs of my Swan patients, in the hospital unit, I managed to bring up, successfully, two years' broods of orphaned Cygnets, during the time at Costessey. We had between thirty and forty of these babies to bring up every year. The success rate proved better at the sanctuary, for Cygnets, as they obviously had a more natural environment than they had been able to enjoy at the old cottage, at Sparham. Unless you can give a Cygnet aquatic vegetation, reeds, natural banks to walk in and out of the water, it is unwise and, in our opinion, cruel to attempt raising an orphaned Cygnet. He will usually die at an early age, sadly deformed in his limbs, through rickets, caused by undernourishment and lack of essential vitamins and minerals needed to promote healthy growth. He will never reach the size of a proper, wild, river Swan.

On the river a Cygnet is constantly moving, travelling great distances for his size, fighting against the currents, and battling to keep up with his parents. In the confines of a back garden, it is impossible to emulate this, so his developing muscles never get the adequate exercise needed. You end up with a tame Swan, the size of a goose, never really fit enough for release. This has only been learnt by us after many trials, and much bitter experience. The Costessey Cygnets were the biggest, least tame and straight boned. The sanctuary had space, good food and some grazing.

Releasing them, when the time comes, is still one of the hardest things I had to do. There comes a time when you have to let them go. Knowing the dangers they would have to face, from fishing tackle, pollution, boats and power cables in their sky, makes releasing unbearable. But you cannot keep them all. After all we had only fifteen acres, and over four hundred Swans, by this time. More Swans were coming in all the time. Len has explained, earlier in this book, the impossibility of obtaining land for our Swans. Eddie, incidently, was once severely admonished for daring to release a fit Swan back upon the land from which he came. The land, and in fact, thousands of acres of this part of England, was, and is, owned by the RSPB!

So when the time came, when the Cygnets were a year old, I would release them onto a river. The feeling of abandonment would overwhelm me. They had never known big water, most were still tiny when rescued and brought to the hospital, with their fishing tackle injuries. Many, in fact, refused to leave, so I would push them away and they would run, squeaking straight back to me, or the car. I would stay with them, until they accepted their fate and I would drive away, feeling only loss and guilt.

Hate would well up inside me toward the so called sportsmen who had caused this problem in the first place.

Photos: Pierre Gleizes, Paris.

As has been explained, power cables kill thousands of Swans each year in the British Isles. Those who are not lucky enough to have been killed outright, suffer many sorts of injuries, bone fractures being the most common – wings and legs are broken. Some of these injuries can mend by strapping or splinting, wing injuries that is. The splints being left in place for several weeks. Or, in some instances, surgical pinning is carried out. It must be remembered, however, that if a huge bird, like a Swan, has collided with a power cable and falls to the ground, he will almost certainly have suffered internal injuries.

Many well meaning people, usually within animal welfare, are unaware of this fact, and in their haste to have the visible wound attended to, will immediately lift the Swan. As with a human victim of a road traffic accident, to move the Swan will obviously cause greater suffering, if not handled carefully. So, as with the human victim, a stretcher is used, usually by a very experienced ambulance crew. So then with the Swan. We had designed special Swan stretchers and used these, always, successfully. Another stressful practice to avoid is the understandable, and yet incorrect, decision to rush the injured Swan to the vets for immediate examination and treatment. Worse when operations are carried out before the Swan has even recovered from the shock of the collision. The injured Swan, with possible spinal injuries, would have obviously been driven to the vet in the back of a car. Imagine doing this to an injured human. Following treatment the Swan then has to be transported, sometimes over distances of many miles, to a bird care establishment. All these movements, can and do, unduce haemorrhaging to an internal wound.

Through experience, we have been shown it is better, and certainly far kinder, to avoid movement of a Swan found under a power cable, as far as is possible. If the Swan has to be transported, a thick pad of foam is essential to gently place the Swan upon. He should then be left in a secluded pen area, quietness being paramount. Simple dressing or strapping is obviously acceptable, and cleaning wounds of blood, owing to the ever present risk of the wound becoming fly blown. Should the Swan survive a period of at least a week, only then should major surgery be considered.

The second most common injury, from power cable collisions, are leg breakages. We have achieved great success with these, by our own tried and tested method, commonly known as benign neglect. In the early days we tried splinting, strapping or plaster casts. None of these were successful. Many times the leg would swell, and infection set in, and death would follow from gangrene. The Swan, unable to go into the water, would become dirty and soiled with his own excrement. Some vets now pin legs, which means major surgery and unnecessary stress.

There is one simple method, with which we have had a 100% success rate. That is to let the Swan go into the water! The Swan will swim, happily, the water will take the weight of his body and the broken

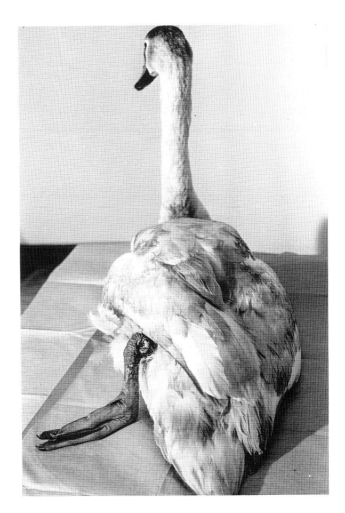

leg, will heal, with time. With easy access to a food bowl, supplied, this had proven all that is necessary. Just a safe place, food and time.

A Swan showed us this, the credit cannot go to us. We rescued her from a golf course in Beccles, Suffolk. She had three fractures in one leg and we were unable to attempt splinting, as one break was too high up the leg into the body. We decided to put her in our therapy pond, with our other Swans. We believed she should be with her Swan friends, for what we thought would be her last few days of life. Then, a few days later, she limped out of the pond, using the steepest exit bank! In a few more days, she was hobbling around the garden. Soon after, she started practising short take-off flights, using her now mended, though crooked, leg. Then she actually flew, up and over the hospital. She landed back into the pond and stayed for another couple of days. Then she disappeared. She must have chosen freedom. We wished her well and thanked her for showing us how to mend a broken leg. Leave it alone!

Although this method had proven successful for us, many times, the ultimate proof came when I managed to pursuade a veterinary nurse, calling for advice, from Scotland, to try our treatment on a Swan they had in their care. Not only did they follow my advice to the letter but, the lady caring for the Swan, actually dug a pond in her garden for the therapy needed. A few months later we received a call, from Scotland, telling us that the leg had healed and the Swan had been successfully released.

Isle of Bute Swan and Nearly My Swan Song

Whilst pushing the wheelbarrow full of wheat through the, now, very deep furrows across the marsh, I began suffering sharp pains in my stomach. The pains at times became so unbearable, I had to stop and bend over the barrow, water exuding from my eyes, tears of frustration and pain at being stopped from going about my chores. I would shrug the pain off, more often than not, as there were too few hours in the day to do so much work, for a creature suffering far more than I.

Sometimes if the wheelbarrow sunk too deep, when pushing it, I would turn and pull it instead. One way or another, I got the Swans fed. The walk from the river, with the water bottles, was probably even more difficult to manage. When Eddie, in between his maintenance work and water pumping or cleaning ponds, spotted me struggling, he would rush to my rescue. More often than not, we were too engrossed in our own chores, rushing around, trying to get all Swans fed and watered, before being called out, on the inevitable rescue.

So my tummy pains were ignored and the days turned into months of discomfort.

One evening, I was visiting Len and Sheila, at their cottage, when a call came from the Isle of Bute, off mainland Scotland, over four hundred miles away from us. The caller had rescued the Swan from a loch (lake) and was in need of help. It had apparently been sick for some while and was now completely lethargic. So much so, that our Scottish friend, the local warden, simply had to pick the Swan up, and take it home.

Unable to find anyone to help in Scotland, he found our telephone number, in a Birdwatcher's book. Sheila, Len and I, looked at each other, wondering what we could do. I volunteered to go, and decided to try the journey, in my tired ancient Ford Escort. After all, this was not really a rescue, so did not require Len's fully equipped ambulance. It was usual for me to do the pick-ups, as we called them, when the caller already had the Swan in care. So on that cold, black, February evening, I set out for Scotland. I had persuaded Len and Sheila it would be quicker driving overnight, and it meant I would only be away from the sanctuary for one whole day. Ever faithful Eddie would cover for me. Len would do the treatments.

After a slow, hard, drive for the first few hours, in thick fog, I was approaching Carlisle when the tummy cramps became extremely uncomfortable. I felt as if I had been inflated and needed, desperately, to stand up and stretch. I drove into Carlisle and thought I would look for a café, or possibly a bed and breakfast house, so I would be alone with my pain.

Nothing was open. It was about four a.m. I drove on again but the pain worsened. I eventually reached Gretna Green, on the Scottish border, the pain now was impossible to endure. I found a hotel and panicking, wrapped on the old front door. No answer. It was still too early in the morning. I found a phone box that still worked, a rarity in Britain, spoke to Len and told him I was very sick but would try to carry on to the Isle of Bute. Having now travelled too far to turn back, I had no choice but to carry on.

I arrived at Greenock for the ferry to the Island later that morning. I was now in a terrible state and knew I just could not go on. Unable to make the ferry trip, I phoned the warden and asked if he would bring the Swan to me. He kindly agreed, so I instructed him on how to wrap and secure the sick Swan. I huddled in the car, now doubled up with pain. I thought I would try and sleep while I waited for the arrival of the ferry. Wishful thinking told me I would wake up and the pain would be gone. Before sleep came, however, the ferry arrived. Thanking the warden I settled my Swan in the back of the Escort. She sat quietly. I was now wondering how on earth I was going to manage the depressingly long journey back to Norfolk. I knew I could not do it. In fact the only thing I did achieve was a phone call back to Norfolk, explaining my predicament. They suggested, quite rightly, I should get to a hospital and they would send somebody up to help me. This seemed a good idea. My Swan was quiet and content in the back of the car and, at least in hospital, I would be able to stretch out, and rest before the journey home. I was directed to the hospital in Greenock. Leaving the Swan in the car park, I entered.

I do not remember much more after that. It all happened so quickly. I remember a doctor asking, how long had my stomach been so big? Was I pregnant? Pretty difficult for a Swan loving celibate, I laughed! He told me they would have to operate.

Next thing I remember was a nurse looking at me. Before I had barely come round from the anaesthetic, she was telling me that I needed a shower.

"But what has happened to me, what was wrong, stop pulling me, I don't want a shower."

Too late. My cotton robe was off, I was in the shower – still groggy. Maybe the nurse just did not like the smell of Swans? After this abrupt awakening, I asked a gentler nurse how my Swan was coping. She told me the Swan had been the centre of attention and was perfectly all right, sitting in the car. The hospital had received a phone call telling them someone was on their way from Norfolk, to pick up my Swan. Now quite relieved I slipped back into the uneasy sleep I had been so roughly awakened from.

Obtaining information about your own body is very difficult, I was to discover. The doctors seemed far too busy to explain and the nurses didn't seem to know much. I found out more by phoning my mum, who is an expert at breaking through the barriers of medical jargon. She told me I had had a malignant tumour and some personal bits and pieces removed. Apparently, I should have had it seen to much sooner.

"But the Swans needed me," I told her.

The Virus

It would take me some time to get back to full strength, after my operation, so Len and Eddie continued to cover for me.

Giving daily injections was a task that had befallen me, from necessity on the Swans part and Len's desire that I should – as I had spent many hours reading veterinary medical books and desperately trying to catch up with the knowledge, I felt I must have, if I wanted to help a particular species. I cannot work any other way.

The following is an account of what have been the worst days of my life. If I had already promised Woody that I would give my life to the Swans, this episode would have concreted my dedication to them, for the suffering that my closest Swan friends were put through.

These next pages are dedicated, then, to Woody.

We had a phone call from the owners of an stately home, here in East Anglia.

"Come and move the bloody lot, they're a damn nuisance," they demanded.

"We don't want them here!"

They had on their lake a whole family of Trumpeter Swans. These beautiful creatures are normally only found in the wild of North America. Also, unfortunately, within the prison camps of wildfowl dealers. Apparently these Swans had been bought with the house. The new owners not realising that they had been purchased as an adornment for the lake. They had been bought and sold off, like so many bricks or stones. Coming from a wildfowl dealer they had all, obviously, been pinioned.

They had been purchased when the five Cygnets were tiny, and now they were fully grown, having reached their first year. The parents were ready to mate again, it now being springtime, so were obeying the rules of millions of years of evolution. They were now trying to chase these yearling Swans away. Being flightless, it was not possible for them to leave so, they were being badly beaten, one in particular lying forlornly on the bank, in a very poor way.

The whole family were brought to the sanctuary, much against our usual rule, of only rescuing wild Swans. We try not to aid and abet this totally immoral pastime of purchasing birds. This should have died out with its equivalent, slavery. However, we have always been a "soft touch" for people who do not want to spend their money. Ours being an unpaid, voluntary service. Clearing up for people had become

our lot but, as long as it was helping a Swan, we fell for it.

After the Trumpeter family had been with us for a week, the smallest yearling, who had been lying on the bank of the lake, at the mansion, became very ill. She stopped eating, could not move, and had difficulty passing her toilet. Two days later she died and we sent her body to the Veterinary Investigation Centre, of the Ministry of Agriculture, for post mortem examination. While we awaited the results other Swans, that were close to the family, started showing similar symptoms. We were very anxious. We rang the Ministry and asked if they had any results yet, to which they said they were doing further tests, but had we lost any ducks?

We said we had not.

Then one of the sick Swans died, in the hospital unit. Next day another. They, too, were sent hurriedly for post mortem. It can take some time for the results to come back, the waiting was traumatic. We did not know what to do. The symptoms at this time seemed similar to those for Aspergillosis, but it was the terrible trouble when trying to pass faeces, that worried me. I noticed that the faeces was not normal but consisted only of a runny, yellow tinged liquid. I kept watching my patients, while Len read and read, wondering what on earth it could be. I scrubbed and disinfected everything in and around the hospital and, thank goodness, isolated the Swans in this area, suspecting this sickness might be contagious.

Eventually the result came through, from the Ministry, for the young Trumpeter. They said she had died of a Virus. Her liver and kidneys were covered in white nodules. In some places holes had perforated the oesophagus and food had been passing through these, which accounted for her reasonable weight. Of particular significance was the condition of her cloaca, which was black and friable, as though it had been burnt. This accounted for the obvious pain the yearling suffered when passing its faeces. The post mortem report named the Virus as DVE (Duck Virus Enteritis). We read up on it. Everything we read said the Virus would wipe out every duck and goose in the vicinity. As we had not seen a dead duck or goose, several were flying in and out, we were perplexed. We had only Swans dying. Were the Ministry right? After a while more results came back from the Ministry, they stated that the last two Swans had died of the same Virus.

"How can this be?" we asked the pathologist.

"That's what our tests conclude," he said.

Continuing, "I will have to come and see you at the sanctuary."

Meanwhile, more Swans in the unit were becoming ill and I nursed them all. Every one was a personal friend. They were all Swans I had been treating, every day, and now they were all dying, one by one, in each hospital pen.

Every inside patient had by this time died, and I put the last few, from the original thirty, in the outside hospital pens, into one, all together. I believed each pen to be contaminated.

My nightmare had started. It was in full swing. Each day I would go to my hospital and find another Swan dying. I stayed with every one, during their last, agonising moments. They suffered the most horrendous pain I have ever witnessed, up to this very day. I had no thought of the personal risk I was taking, being so close. I didn't care. I was losing everything that mattered to me.

The pathologist arrived and asked to be shown around. He knew Len well, so we took him around while he asked questions.

"You will have to get rid of the ducks," he said.

"But why?" we asked. "None of them have died and they have been in with the sick Swans."

"Never mind that, get rid of them."

"Shoot them do you mean?" we asked.

"Up to you, and release all the Swans."

"It sounds too risky," we said. "We do not know how this thing is spread."

"I can't tell you that either, but you've got no choice, they will all die."

"But we'll spread it to the wild Swans on the river, won't we?"

No answer came.

"Oh, and put foot baths around, you must dip your wellingtons before you leave the sanctuary, and wear overalls and rubber gloves," he said, then he left, adding, "Let me know if any more Swans die."

We could not understand how we could be told to release the Swans and yet carry out the strict safety precautions recommended. It made no sense. We ignored his advice to release the Swans. How could we risk the lives of other Swans? We would make sure that any Swans within the vicinity of another who had died of the virus, was isolated. We certainly were not going to shoot wild ducks, flying in and out, either. But we did supply foot baths and I became meticulous, concerning my hygiene, and wore disposable overalls.

I continued to nurse each Swan. It was too late for me now if it was contagious to humans. The Ministry had mentioned the similarity, of the Swan Virus, to that of the Herpes strain. I left Eddie to feed the main flock of disabled Swans on the lake and the pairs, in their breeding pens, far away at the back of the sanctuary. My feeding chores stopped now. No more daily treatments. All my patients around the hospital had died, all thirty of them. I devoted my time,

Photo: Pierre Gleizes, Paris.

Photo: Pierre Gleizes, Paris.

during this, to being with them. My presence seemed all I could give them. I could not ease their pain.

One morning, my hospital Swans gone, I ventured to the dyke pen where Swans, recovering after treatment, were placed. Two Swans were hiding in a dark corner, in the water, by a high, overgrown bank. Dislike of light (photophobia), being a symptom noticed with previous infected Swans. They were very quiet and did not take any notice of my presence, unlike the others, who all looked at me expecting their food. I noticed the sick Swans had strange shaped necks. They were at an angle, unlike any other I had seen before. I got to know this appearance so well and would recognise it, immediately, to this day. The Swans seemed to seek the dark and groaned every time they passed faeces. My heart sank. Not them too, I cried. No, no, it can't be. Woody's in there. And King Kenneth. And Little Baby, a very dear Swan, who loved being fussed by me. Not you too, I cried.

I thought that if we took the two sick looking Swans from the water, the others may stand a chance. Desperate, possibly in vain, but I must try. Eddie had to help me. We put them in the hospital pen.

They died only hours later, in exactly the same way the others had. I cried for each one. Eddie said I mustn't, he was desperately upset too, but was fearing for me. I was beyond help. My babies were dying.

That was the beginning of the end, for all my patients of the last eighteen months. Of injections and dressings and therapy and nursing.

Next day, two more Swans were in the dark corner just the same. Eddie helped me again to take them out. They, too, died later that day. My worst fears were confirmed. Every Swan in that dyke pen was likely to be infected, if kept close together. I was determined to try and beat the spread of this evil Virus. There were about sixty five Swans, in this one pen, so I watched, looking for the first sign of sickness. I became an expert at recognising this disease, or whatever it was.

One thing we were sure of – it was not Duck Virus Enteritis. All the ducks and geese were still alive and well.

While I stayed with my Swans, Len was phoning around the world, trying to find someone to help. He had found out, though, that there was not a vaccination available, in England, that we could have used to treat Swans and so help to avoid the spread of the Virus. He contacted a well known pathologist in Saskatchewan, Canada, who had been studying incidents of DVE in wild waterfowl. He was certain of only one thing, that if our trouble was indeed DVE, we would lose every duck or Canada goose in the area. It seemed we were right in not accepting the Ministry's report. We did not, for one minute, suspect subversion, nor deceit, on their part. Simply, they did not know what our Swans were suffering from. They had probably never come across it before. They, at any rate, were unable to offer us any further advice and so, as it always was, with us and the Swans, we had to make our own decisions on what was best for them.

I was terrified for the safety of the Swans either side of the pen where they were now dying, at a steady rate of two or three every day. A new idea came forward, from Len's younger brother, Bob. He was helping us, in those days, and was doing absolutely brilliant work on the effects of lead poisoning in Swans. Though he, like me, has trouble sometimes stringing a sentence together when talking, borders on genius, and we and the Swans will be forever grateful for the work he did. Bob suggested we should move the remaining forty or so Swans, still in the dyke pen, to an empty paddock on the sanctuary, away from the other Swans. A pen had to be erected quickly and Bob advised surrounding it with lime, which will kill all bacteria. So we set to the task, Eddie, Len, Bob and myself. We completed the pen within the day and set about catching the Swans.

I still could not believe what was happening and kept watching the Swans, trying not to single out Woody. But Woody kept watching me too.

It was, of course, easy to see why the Swans had started dying in the dyke pen too. This was the pen into which I put the Swans after they had completed their treatment in the hospital unit. Obviously, then, the Virus stemmed from there, but how? Only one case being an exception, a pair of Swans were in a totally separate dyke pen – they too died, showing the same symptoms as the others. How could this be, as all Swans on either side of them were unaffected. We are still unable to account for this phenomenon.

To this day we suspect, that this Virus was intentionally given to our Swans – possibly one Swan only in the hospital unit, from whence it spread upon its evil journey. As the young Trumpeter was the first to die, it must be presumed she was the first Guinea Pig, victim, or whatever, that most insidious, warped, scientific brained thing, would have called her. A natural virus would have, surely, spread throughout the entire sanctuary, killing every Swan. There is no way the Swans next to the dyke pen could have escaped it. We have our suspicions but no proof – as yet. One night, however, I did disturb someone around the hospital unit using a torch, they disappeared into the darkness as Eddie and I reached the unit, the fact that I saw a torch, which was switched off as we approached, and whoever it was, can only really mean one thing. Many animals and birds have been, and still are, used as Guinea Pigs in scientific research. Many men, demented humans, have furthered their careers, obtained massive grants in the name of science by using animals.

Were our Swans a perfect "control" batch? We certainly had the ideal setup for just an experiment. Nowhere else in the world could there be found such a convenient population of mute Swans.

Was it really all just a coincidence?

Bob Baker's new lime circled pen became the last home for all the Swans that were put into it. One by one, day by day, they would die. I spent all the daylight hours with them. Every day I donned my overalls, boots and gloves, looking like something recently escaped from a Nuclear Power station.

My patients were suffering, so I would suffer with them. They were always, and always will be, more than just patients, of course, but that is emotive. We at Swan Rescue Service are very often accused of this. As Len has stated, earlier in this book, to be emotional and to be British is considered a crime. I am unashamedly guilty.

The day came – Woody fell ill. His eyes stared, with that unforgettable look of pain, his neck, in that terrible arched position. He groaned with pain as he excreted that foul, yellow tinged liquid. I sat with him and held his head till he found peace. One day, I will meet you again, dear friend. I will find out, before I leave this place, who did this to you and your friends.

We needed, desperately, access to an electron microscope. Bob and Len wanted to see exactly what this virus, or whatever, looked like. They took samples of mucus and faeces. The local university would not allow use of their microscope. There were only a few Swans left in the isolation pen now, but we had to know more. Was it a virus, or was it bacteria in the water? It seemed to thrive in water, possibly food bowls. Or was it passed from Swan to Swan by feather lice or mites, such as the evil Myxomatosis?

Ninety nine Swans in all died. This number is indelibly printed on my brain, forever. I nursed, alone, every one of them. Nothing can ever be as bad as those days. I pray I never have to see suffering like that again.

So the virus ended. Not one duck or goose ever died. The other Swans remained unaffected.

Bob is still helping Swans. Thankyou Bob for trying.

RINA MILSOM

111

PART III

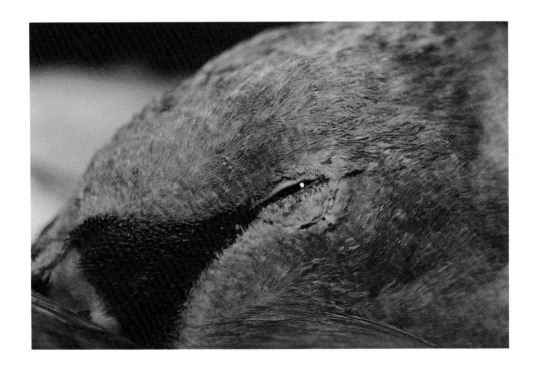

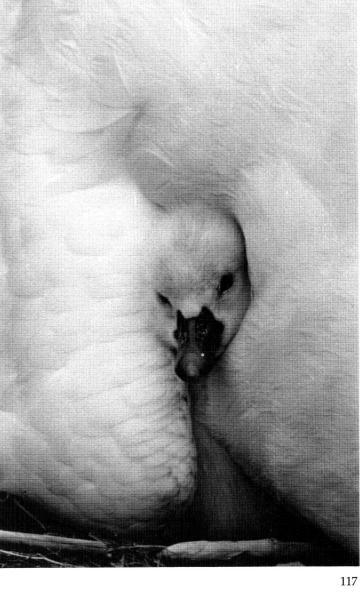

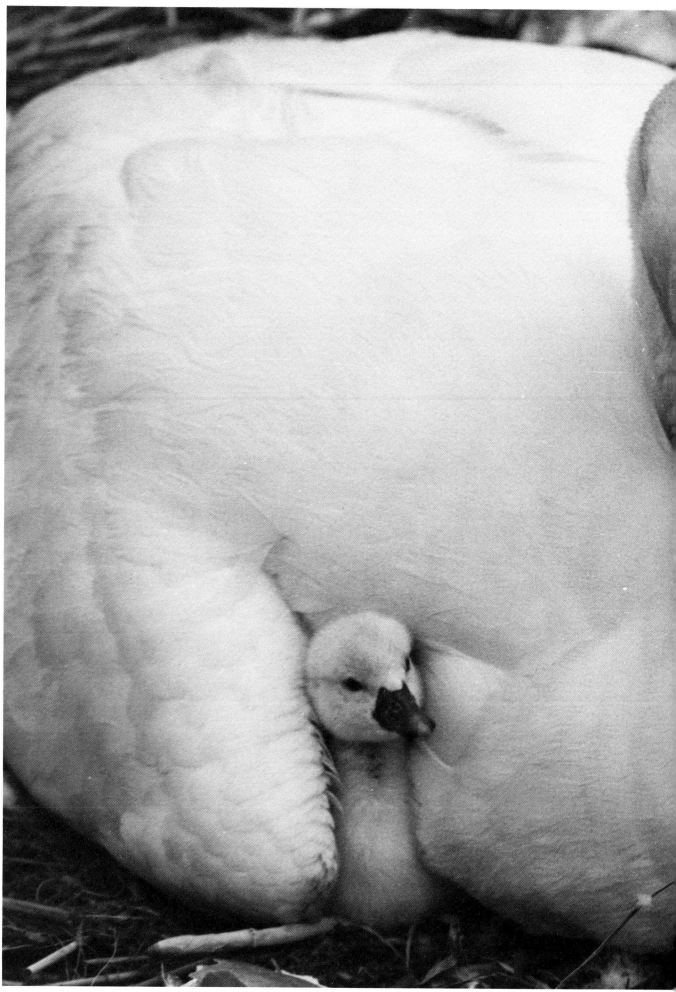

Old Swan patient checking out new arrivals.

CHAPTER 10
Still Searching

With the amount of publicity we had given the Swans, aided by the insatiable appetite of the media, we were now spending a lot of time answering questions, received by mail, from many countries – but never from anyone concerned with animal welfare in England. Veterinary surgeons were an exception, most of them eager for any information regarding treatments. Wild bird care not being on the curriculum at most veterinary colleges. There is no money in it.

Our Swan story was featured in magazine articles in many countries, covered in the international issue of the *Readers Digest* and we had now appeared on over fifty television interviews. We had been heard by millions of people all over the British Isles through over one hundred radio broadcasts, campaigning for the Swans.

However, we were not, and never have been, recognised nor accepted by any authority in the United Kingdom, therefore receiving no credibility.

Could it be that the reason for the total refusal by the peoples of power, to recognise our existence, was because of their guilt? We think so. Our very existence, the fact that we were doing our job and doing it well obviously meant that the people and organisations paid to care for Britain's wildlife, were not doing their job? Proof that they still are not, is the amazing amount of voluntary rescue centres and wildlife hospitals that exist. You would think that receiving no help or encouragement from the pur-ported animal welfare establishments, was enough. They added insult to injury by harassing us. The threats of raids on your premises, by uniformed inspectors, were a continual "thorn in the side". Ironical, when all you were trying to do was to stop an animal suffering. With the ability to attract publicity for your cause and with the added blessing of being able to use these opportunities to the full, only alienated the already established organisations. Here is where our old friend "ego" comes in, add to this gross embarrassment and you have a recipe for disaster.

When we travelled around Norfolk on local res-cues, we could not help but be amazed by the vast amount of land, in that country, that appeared to be unused – especially North Norfolk. The land not owned by the Crown, is still enormous in size and ideal Swan land. We were continually asked by supporters why we had never approached land-owners for help in acquiring space for the Swans. We had tried, but people thought that we had not tried hard enough. To satisfy them, I made a recording of one such telephone request for land. The owner of this particular land is a "titled" gentleman. He has more acres of land than you could count. Some of it being ideal Swan land. It has everything that a Swan needs, rivers, dykes, grazing, aqua vegetation, and hardly any power cables. It is, in short, Swan paradise, and could accommodate, without any fear of overcrowding, three to four thousand Swans. This, then, taken from the cassette tape in the answer machine was that conversation:

"Hello Lord so and so?"
"Yes."
"My name is Baker."
"Oh yes."
"Len Baker."
"Oh."
"I was wondering if I could come and talk with you?"
"What about?"
"Swans."
"Beg your pardon?"
"Swans."
"What about them?"
"Well, we need your help."
"Oh really?"
"Yes."
"What help do you want?"
"We need space."
"What do you need space for?"
"For our Swans."
"Oh yes, you're that Swan chappie aren't you?"
"Yes."
"Good, I was going to call you." Excitement welled up inside me.
"Yes, can you and your people get up here and remove these bloody Swans, they are eating the tops off my carrots."
"They what?"
"Bloody things are a nuisance."
"We cannot, and do not remove Swans unless they are injured!" (A fact of law.)
"Well I'll make sure the bloody things are injured." I replaced the telephone.

This sort of conversation was commonplace, when begging the British aristocracy for help, it is under-standable by us at least. The aristocracy was spawned from a long line of plundering Empire builders, who had, by raping and overpowering other weaker nations, obtained the resources needed to establish wealth. The Commonwealth?

And our supporters thought that they would help a Swan?

The gardens at Lathe Green were filling with

Swans at an alarming rate. This problem was exacerbated by our rescuing a group of oiled covered Swans from Ipswich Docks. This was a regular occurrence. Ipswich Docks being managed by two authorities whose answer to all problems regarding water quality and pollution of the dock water, was to blame each other. While they, like children at play time, argued over who was responsible, we usually cleared up the worst of the oil and took the Swans, bathed them, kept them the usual few weeks, and when completely waterproof, returned them to the docks.

Returning Swans back to their site of rescue is imperative. This is an unfortunate fact of life. If you leave areas devoid of Swan flocks, other Swans desperately seeking space, will land. Consequently, even more Swans will suffer.

Before the instigation of the Swan Rescue Service many Ipswich Swans would die, by drowning, after being covered in oil. At one time we rescued, over a non stop period of eleven hours, forty two oiled Swans. Seven of these died and we released the rest back to the docks. They were oiled again six weeks later, this time nine died. So it goes on at Ipswich Docks, and other docks, to this day.

There appears to be, somewhere out there upon the high seas, a mystical, magical ship's Captain, he is of course, Greek. He apparently discharges sump oil into Ipswich Docks at every visit and then disappears into thick sea mist, before anyone can get the name or number of his ship. That's what the authorities at Ipswich Docks tell us anyway!

Their story, however, does not seem to have about it, that ring of truth. It is made even more suspect, by the fact that many people, residents of Ipswich, and ex employees of the dock area, insist that the oil comes from piping just below the quay, and is in fact the result of badly policed environmental problems and ancient, damaged pipes, running from factories and industrial units beneath the quay. The owners of the factories surrounding Ipswich Docks, are good rate payers. You must not upset rate payers!

If on a summer's evening, you go for a pleasant walk to look at the little boats, moored and coming and going at Foxes Marina in Ipswich, and you breathe the fresh, clean air, the hairs in your nostrils will shrivel from the effects of diesel oil. Try it, I am sure you will find it quite invigorating! Study the surface of the water, enjoy the beautiful rainbow colours created by the mixing of diesel oil, sump oil, detergent and ethylene glycol. The colours and spectacle seen would stimulate the would-be Monets and Turners amongst you. An added bonus, if you are really lucky, are dead Gulls and fish. But the authorities that control the water quality at Ipswich tell us that this is untrue. Who are we to argue? They after all, the Anglian Water Authority and the Port Authority, are experts.

Oiled Swans are always a pathetic and sadly moving sight. The natural thing for any bird to do, when its feathers are soiled, is to preen. It then swallows the oil. The extensive damage is done to the precious mucous lining of the oesophagus and gut.

The toxic, acidic nature of oil, also damages liver and kidney. The last thing we worried about, consequently, was the damage to the plumage. After giving the treatment to alleviate internal damage, we would watch the faeces to see whether oil or blood was present, only then would we bath the Swan.

We built a special Swan bath and installed a thermostatically controlled shower unit. The temperature set at exactly forty one degrees centigrade. A cheap proprietary dishwashing liquid was always used, as cheaper liquids do not contain lanolin. After a complete soaking with the warm water, the liquid was applied directly onto the soiled feathers and worked through them and down to the skin. We let the Swan sit in its own bath water, this allowed the usually badly soiled stomach area to soak, whilst we worked on the plumage.

After emptying the bath of soiled water, the Swan is sprayed until droplets of water form upon the plumage, thus ensuring that waterproofing has returned. The spray head held in such a position as to make sure the water jets rinse away any remaining detergent from the quill end of the feathers, down to the broad end.

We achieved great success with this method and bathed many hundreds of Swans and other birds. If a Swan adult was a stressful and difficult task to undertake, then imagine a two day old Cygnet with no feathers, just down. Most of these, however, succumbed to the effects of the oil before we arrived on the scene, it then being a matter of carcase removal and concentration on the parent Swans.

When Swans have been bathed and rinsed they are put outside, in a special area, after at least three or four nights in their heated indoor drying pens. The outside area has access to a clean pond, and the Swans would bathe and preen until natural waterproofing was present. There are those who believe that the preen gland, in front of the tail and on top of it, is of some significance. It is wrongly understood that the Swan takes oil from the gland, and rubbing it with its beak into its plumage renders the Swan waterproof. This is not so. The gland does indeed contain oil but waterproofing is achieved through air entrapment within, and beneath, feathers and down. Continual preening ensures this. The amount of oil excreted by the preen gland is so minute, that it is thought to be used as a final, very quick embellishment, rather than a waterproofing agent.

The food of choice for recuperating oiled Swans is bread, enabling absorption and consequent excretion of any remaining oil within the gut.

At the time of writing, a new rivers management authority was launched. As with politicians, promises of competent river management remain to be proven. The waterbirds and fishes of Britain hope they are capable. So do we.

So then, oil slicks, power cable collisions, fishing tackle injuries, lead poisoning, chemical pollution, poisoning from toxic crops, e.g. oil seed rape, poison from organo phosphorus and dieldrin from over zealous and incorrectly formulated spraying and road

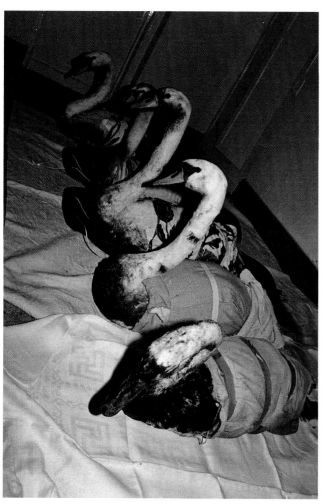
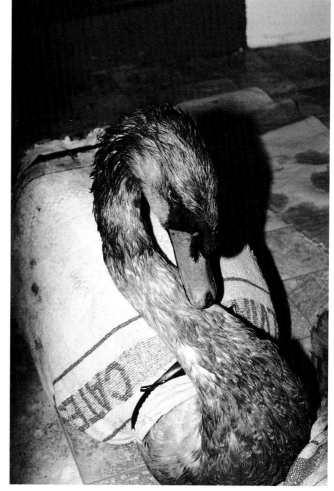

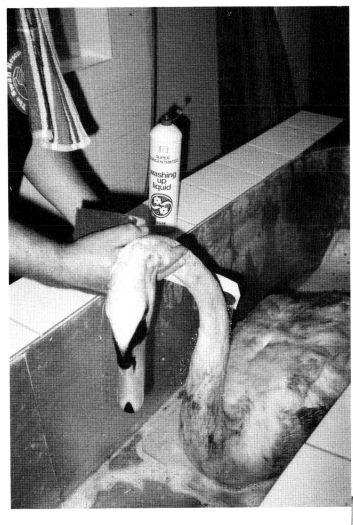

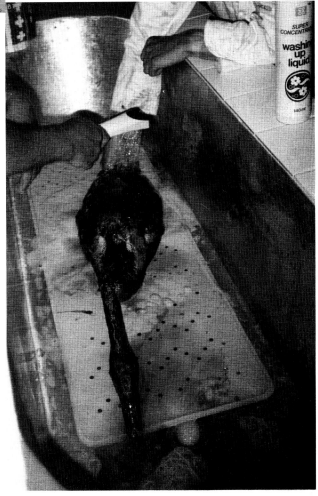

traffic accidents. What else can befall that creature of tradition, myth and beauty?

People. Perverted human beings. Acts of vandalism, so perverse in fact, that even we, after witnessing them, still cannot believe them. Here are a few.

Boiling golden syrup poured over Swans, air gun shootings, shot gun attacks, crossbow attacks, piercing by dartboard darts, crucifixion by crossbow bolts to the trunk of a tree, cutting the throat twelve times with a carving knife, attempts to sever a beak with a sheath knife, lassoing and towing behind boats, decapitation by machete, force feeding of lead weights by scientists, mass shootings by farmers and on and on.

Why? One reason being that the Swan is large, white and an easy target. He is approachable and, what is worse, has been taught by ordinary, nice people, with their tit bits of food, to trust human beings. On any day, near any lake, pond or river, you will see people feeding waterbirds. It is a habit, tradition if you will. People love to feed animals, it makes them feel good. We are all guilty of this harmless, in itself, pastime. Sadly not all human beings are harmless.

When we try to explain to dear little old ladies and the like, that it is kinder to leave wildlife alone to be wildlife, we are regarded as hard and accused of not loving animals. You cannot blame them. Some of them have indeed purchased bird tables from bird societies, whilst paying their yearly subscriptions. Having a hundred years standing, the bird society has much credibility, so obviously know better than us.

We should not need to buy the quaint little thatched bird tables to encourage wild birds into our gardens but should ensure that the birds have a plentiful supply of natural food. One well known bird society is now selling berry bearing shrubs and bushes to its subscribers. This deserves our applause.

A tame bird or animal, tamed through our kindness, becomes a vulnerable creature, awaiting the attention of the sort of cretin that inflicted the suffering upon some of our white friends, you see depicted in this book.

At Martham near Great Yarmouth there lived, on the river Thurne, a delightful family of Swans well known to us. They were, unfortunately, also well known amongst the local people. Because of their friendliness they were the subjects of a tragic fate.

A farmer phoned to tell us he had seen the Cob of the family flying very low over his dyke, crying. He could hear this clearly. Beneath the Cob were the rest of his family, all dead in the water of the dyke. His family consisted of his mate and four Cygnets.

We have in the past collected groups of dead Swans, but they have usually died from poisoning. X-ray examinations, though, on this family told us a different story. All except the Cob, were blasted to death by a man, allegedly from a nearby village. The weapon used was a twelve bore shotgun. This was discharged at a very close range, shown by the penetration of shot upon post mortem.

Air rifle attack – Stafford.

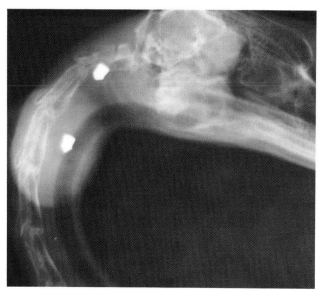

X-ray of above – operation successful.

Living in the country the sound of guns was not unexpected nor unusual. Being so familiar, it does not normally warrant investigation. This was obviously so on the fateful Sunday at Martham. The Swan family would leave the water and unfortunately, were regularly fed by a very kind gentleman every morning, at a certain hour. This morning it was not their friend that met them with white sliced bread, it was a known poacher and his gun.

The story of this tragedy received much publicity, us offering a reward for information leading to the conviction of the killer. Many phone calls came and one man in particular, from Martham, gave us the name and address of the poacher responsible. This, together with the X-rays, we gave to the Caistor Police station. Nothing happened. This, after many such cases passed to the police by us, and not resulting in any action by them, was not at all surprising. You have to actually witness the killing, if your story is to be considered. According to the boys in blue in Norfolk, this is the law. At least it is when wildlife are the victims.

The lone Cob, sole survivor of this too trusting family, is probably out there somewhere still.

This then is what can happen, when, because of interference by the continual development of our countryside environment, pursuades, indeed forces wild creatures closer to human beings to beg food essential for survival. The worst crime we are guilty of, it seems to us at Swan Rescue Service, is to turn the creatures of the wild, through kindness and concern, into creatures that are tame and therefore vulnerable.

marsh. With Eddie living so close, this marsh received proper and frequent management, Eddie bringing home piles of discarded fishing tackle regularly. It was not, however, fishing tackle that was responsible for little Bushy's injury. For unknown to Bushy, a mentally deranged youth was on his way, one day, to the marsh with his toy, a crossbow.

The person on the phone told us that there was a Swan on the marsh with something sticking out of its head. Eddie was on the marsh in a matter of minutes to see Bushy, still in the water, with the bolt of a

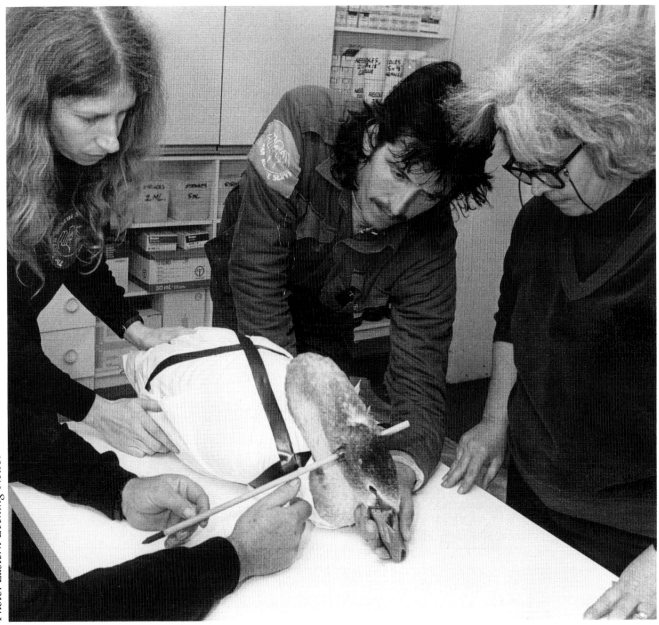

Photo: Eastern Evening News.

Had the Martham family not been imbibed with trust, they would probably still be alive today.

"Bushy" the Cygnet lived on a marsh with his parents, well known to Eddie as it is very close to his home in the sleepy little village near Breydon Water. The village boasts a Roman ruin, some scattered caravan parks and a shop or two. Eddie knows the marsh as you know your living room. Bushy was growing into a Swan at a healthy rate in spite of continual problems with Coarse fishermen upon his

crossbow through his head. Eddie brought his friend home and with trembling hands we withdrew the bolt. It was fourteen inches long. It had pierced Bushy's head, missed the vertebrae by thousandths of an inch just above the oesophagus and trachea and, slightly on passing, damaged the ear cavity. The only thing that had stopped the bolt from passing right through his head, were the flights, which had caught in the cavity.

Bushy went through his ordeal well upon the

surgery table. It was Rina, Sheila, Eddie and I that needed the treatment!

We dressed the holes with antibiotic cream and left them to heal. Bushy was put in an outside dry pen, and within a few days he was put with the other Swans. They accepted him.

Meanwhile we had contacted the police and made the necessary statements. They said they would do what they could. Eddie, however, impatient with the sloth like progress of the police, made his own enquiries, we soon had a name and address. This we passed onto the police. We waited. Nothing happened. Time drifted by – after some weeks had passed, in desperation and frustration, we contacted the police. Their reply was as expected. They were making enquiries.

It must be understood that the Wildlife and Countryside Act is the official act sanctioned and passed by Parliament. The wording of the act is written in the same language of gobbledegook that can be read within the small print on a guarantee of a Taiwanese toaster. It is written, as are most Governmental reports, with the clarity of a foggy day and the ambivalence of a young lady on her first date.

The wording concerning the crossbow bolt through little Bushy's head, contained the phrase "did intentionally cause injury . . ." – "intentionally". So the question obviously asked by the director of prosecution, has to be:

"Did you do that on purpose, or was it an accident?"

"It was an accident." Came the obvious reply.

"I was shooting at a piece of wood I had stuck in the ground for target practice and I didn't know the Swan was there." The case never reached the court.

This, let us not forget, frustrates and annoys the police force as much as it does us. But laws are written, they must go by the book. There are probably many coppers that would like ten minutes or so in some dark corridor with perpetrators of animal and child cruelty. We still have the best police force in the world, in our opinion. We know that the policeman in charge of this case, was on Bushy's side.

Bushy stayed with us for a while and the holes in his head healed into two bright white spots. At least a part, or two parts of Bushy's brown plumage had grown into a real Swan. Bushy flew away.

Crossbows are available from most sports shops or mail order catalogues. Hard to believe, but true.

The list of atrocities committed against Swans also include cases of, what we describe as, "academic vandalism". For example, the case of the idiot bird ringer from Enfield who fitted a ring so high up, on and around the thigh muscle of a Cygnet, that the steel British Trust for Ornithology (BTO) ring cut off the blood supply to the leg and crippled him. He was already suffering the effects of the actions of the bird ringer and, to make matters worse, not being able to swim out of trouble, being hampered by the ring, had the added stress of no less than five assorted fish hooks stuck in various parts of his body, and was also entangled in fishing line with lead weights hanging. Whilst trapped in the water in this condition, he was also stoned. This was in Enfield Town Park. We eventually had to remove the whole family of Swans from the park, they were all suffering from Coarse fishing injuries. The Cygnet injured by the bird ringer died. He at least died under anaesthetic at our veterinary surgeons, undergoing an operation for removal of one of the fish hooks in his stomach. He had simply suffered too much, for too long.

We eventually, after many protests from concerned residents to their local Council offices, managed to secure a ban on Coarse fishing within Enfield Town Park. We hope, for the sake of the waterbirds, and the many dogs who have suffered from fish hooks in the pads of their feet, that this ban will stay in force.

Five fish hooks and crippling B.T.O. ring – Enfield Town Park.

CHAPTER 11
Of Strange Men and Dark Feelings

Returning to Lathe Green from a rescue, one morning in spring, we noticed that a piece of paper had been pinned to the barn door next to our house. It was the usual, official fullscap sheet announcing the fact that planning permission had been applied for the conversion of the farm buildings into dwellings. We could not believe it. The farmer who owned the ruins had offered them to us in the past for a price that was ridiculous. We obviously could not raise the eighty seven thousand pounds he wanted for these relics. But barn conversions were becoming trendy. We were terrified. Would the farmer, in his lust for money, really ruin the world's only Swan hospital? Sure he would. He was a good Tory, an ex Councillor, the "establishment".

The thought of people moving next to the hospice filled us with despair. We drove to the Council offices ironically situated in Swan Lane. Long Stratton. The man at the offices told us we could write a letter stating our objections. We did so. We employed a solicitor and made our objections in the proper manner. We heard nothing. We drove again to the Council offices after a few weeks had passed and met the same young man. He told us that the plans had not actually yet been approved by the Council. We were relieved. He then assured us that he would let us know of any further developments, but this would take some time. He assured us that we need not worry and nothing could be finalised without prior notification, and that we would have our say in the matter when the time was right.

We tried to carry on with our Swan work but this was inhibited by the darkening cloud of uncertainty hovering over the old farmhouse. In our quieter times, we relived the nightmare of the move from the cottage and the marsh at Costessey and, were certain that if the Council had their way and worked to the benefit of the farmer, and their, mutual gain, we would probably lose Lathe Green and with it the Swan Rescue Service. We, however, for the sake of the Swans had to push these depressing thoughts from our minds, but not without wondering who else would have gone through all this for a Swan?

Work, as ever the panacea, took our minds back to where they belonged, with the Swans, and we carried on with the day to day treatments, feeding and fundraising. Spring turned into a hot summer and the hot summer brought with it the fishermen. There seemed to be an incredible increase in the amount of people taking up this sport. This fact is attributed to the ongoing and massive publicity given by the media, in particular Anglia Television. They had secured the services of a local angler and tackle shop proprietor, and a fisherman film director, to make a series of Coarse fishing videos, these to be shown weekly, both regionally and nationally. They were obviously made with the intent of showing the "art"? of the professional Coarse fisherman. It helped the makers of the video when they, after much searching, found an angler who could read and write!

The "sport" became more popular and with an "I'll have some of that" attitude, bored city people appeared on the waterways of East Anglia in their hundreds and, with them beer cans, cigarette packets, crisp packets and bread wrappers, covered the river banks and lakesides of the country. Women even took up the challenge to see if they could catch a bigger fish than their men. It was, and is, a delightful sight, as you can imagine. They seemed to be everywhere, fishing from bridges, boats, jetties, quays, banks, the backs of pick-up trucks, in rivers, lakes, gravel pits, ponds, drainage dykes and puddles. If there is water, it is fished.

Fishing, it seemed to us, had more participants than the Second World War. We have witnessed the dramatic growth of the sport as far afield as Castelnaudary in Southern France and Long Island in the United States. In fact we have cleared discarded fishing tackle from a beach area, in Long Island, frequented by many Swans.

The summer holiday season, here in Norfolk, started on a tragic note, when, on the first day of June, fifteen days before the official start of the Coarse fishing season, an eight year old boy ripped the oesphagus and trachea of a Swan at Somerleyton, causing her unbelievable suffering and death. The weapon that caused her death being a plastic, "just like daddy's", £1.75 toy fishing kit. Perhaps the mother of this particular child now realises the danger, to wildlife, and humans, of a toy like this in the hands of a child. Too late though for the Swan. The season carried on as it had begun.

We are often accused of exaggeration by anglers when stating statistics of waterfowl injured or killed through the activities of some Coarse fishermen. The most popular remark received from them over the years was:

"I have been fishing for twenty or thirty years, I have never seen an injured or dead Swan." The fisherman was probably also a car driver, we wondered how many dead or injured people he had seen scattered over the roadways during his driving career?

Did he think the Swans were immortal?

The reason that not many people had seen dead Swans in the rivers and lakes of East Anglia, over the last twelve years, was simple – we were on site within minutes of all the worst fishing areas of the Norfolk Broads.

The same with power cable deaths. The Electricity Board officers were doubtful that our figures were correct. Not many of their workers had seen dead bodies when out repairing breaks in their cables. Our obvious question, especially when the cable was over a marsh, or adjacent to water, was therefore:

"What broke the cable?"

This question usually went unanswered. There were two reasons why we were quick to remove dead Swans from beneath power cables. First, the risk that other Swans, seeing the dead Swan, would land through the same cable, the dead Swan acting as a decoy. Secondly, there was the risk that a certain company, then established in Norfolk, specialising in the supply of birds for the table, would beat us to the dead Swan. The Swan would end up on a silver platter, at a Cambridge University's May Ball. We believe that this disgusting tradition still continues.

How then, could we prove to the public that there were, indeed, many problems with fishing tackle and power cables? Leave the injured and dead where they were for the doubting public to see? This is not as callous or cruel as it may seem and was to prove a question that would haunt us in the future.

Because we were good at our self appointed jobs as guardians of Britain's Swans, we were, unwittingly, presenting a false image to the public. This being graphically proven when hearing the following conversation. It actually happened at a place known by all at Swan Rescue Service as "Soweto", more properly known as Potter Heigham. Rina and I were getting the gear ready for a rescue at this hell hole for Swans, when he approached, the "know all". He was eating a large ice cream cornet at the time. It was a hot day. I hated the man immediately as I really wanted his ice cream cornet desperately.

"Another one," he asked.

"Yes," I replied. We did not encourage conversation when trying to rescue a Swan. He went on.

"Fishing tackle again?"

"Yes."

"How many today then?"

"Four so far I think." I carried on unstrapping the boat, and Rina was getting impatient to get on with the rescue. Ice cream man carried on.

"Saw your bloke at Stokesby this morning."

"Oh?"

"Saw another one of your team at Acle Bridge."

"Really?" He now moves closer, he was down to the rim of the cone, the soft ice cream melting. One of those delightful chocolate flakes now gone. He continued.

"Who pays you people?" Here we go again.

Without looking at him, now trying to unload the outboard engine, I replied.

"No one." He was shouting now, trying to be heard over the noise of the hire boats.

"Someone must to have all those cars and people on the road." Rina and I lowered the inflatable into the water and threw in the oars, Swan hook and Swan wraps. Motor mouth was annoying me.

"All what cars?" I snapped.

"Well, the wife saw your people at Ranworth and at Salhouse."

"Did she?" I was now trying to start the engine. They never start when people are watching, this attribute being built into Japanese machinery for the Japanese to get their own back on us for some obscure reason. I was dreading the approach of the bored holidaymaker, both hands, palms inwards, thrust into the rear pockets of his jeans, who always seemed to know everything about outboard motors. Ice cream man went on.

"Bloody big organisation, just for Swans init?" The engine fired, through the cloud of blue smoke the ice cream man was now licking the underside of the palm of his hand and his beautiful ice cream cornet was gone.

"There are just two cars, and three of us," I shouted over my shoulder.

"Bugger off," he said, and as a parting remark added, "You must be on a bloody winner!"

We left the quay and ice cream man, and headed down the river Thurne to find our Swan.

We never, incidentally, had more than our two teams on the Norfolk Broads, it was simply that we moved pretty quickly when an injured Swan called.

I have never been a joiner. I am uncomfortable in crowds. The many talks I gave to schools and women's groups were, however, not difficult for me. When confronted by hundreds of children's faces, gazing up at me with expectant expressions, all stage fright disappears. I am lifted to a new height of enthusiasm and find myself ploughing on through my chosen field, with the experience, but definitely not the oral excellence, of an Olivier at the Old Vic. The children want so much, to know and to understand. This is gratifying, for they are our future. They seem to have an insatiable appetite for knowledge pertaining to the animals and the environment. We should encourage this need as often and as much as possible, so as to ensure a better and compassionate understanding for the creatures and plants of the planet.

Lectures, or talks, never flustered me, I am just sorry that I could never find the time to satisfy the many requests, from all over the country, to talk to the children. But the Swans had to come first. Eddie and Rina also took over this task, when time was a problem. Their presence was accepted with alacrity by all.

Our inability to accept invitations for lectures and slide shows, however, gave our supporters and interested conservation groups the untrue and unjust impression that we at Swan Rescue Service were antisocial. This stigma was to last. We could understand and accept the fact that as far as the shooters and fishermen were concerned, we were definitely not "flavour of the month". This was understandable as we would have been very worried indeed if they had attempted to seek our friendship! But not all the aggression shown against us was instigated by these people. The men and women of popular press have caused more damage to us and our lone fight for Britain's Swans, than could be inflicted by a blast from a twelve bore shotgun or a two inch shark hook.

The more blatant these attacks of aggression upon us, the easier we were able to accept them. The sabotaging of our vehicles and boat, the throwing of cow dung at us and our car, were all actions expected by those of lesser brain. We could handle this. It was, and still is, the attacks that come from the uninformed and unenlightened, who act upon rumour and speculation, without having the guts to come and talk with us before publishing their scurrilous drivel. The pen pushers hiding behind the shutters of conformity. Those bored people of the tabloid press and provincial radio and television studio, who, when short of news, start to delve into other people's business hoping to rake up juicy gossip. If you have achieved anything worthwhile you are an obvious subject of their interest. This is perfectly acceptable. Publicity given our Swans has, by and large, only been good for the Swans. But Swans, Rhinos, Gorillas, rain forest trees, or Pandas, do not speak nor write. Hidden behind their pretence of care, it is you, the person, the media are interested in. Readers and viewers cannot easily identify themselves with an animal or a tree. A good "human interest" story sells well, but who, really, is interested in the animal or tree? Being optimistic, we know that thousands are, it's a pity that the media concentrate on personalities. I have been labelled, by the media, as crank, controversial, belligerent, bombastic, radical, provocative, aggressive and eccentric.

I have committed two crimes: I have always marched to the sound of a different drummer and I tried to speak up for the Swans.

Having survived at least some of these attacks of aggression, we have been able to establish a very important fact. That is, although abhorrent and tasteless at the time, they have been merely an affirmation of the credibility of our particular mission. But they are hurtful. It was a child reporter from the *Mail on Sunday* that nearly, very nearly, separated us from the Swans forever. More of this later. Meantime, when dealing with the media, it pays to memorise and use those oft mumbled words, "No comment". Whatever you say, they will print their story. But their ability at producing readable fiction in the columns of the cheaper tabloid newspapers is of no consequence to those of average intelligence, for it surely must be realised that if they were good at their jobs, they would not be working for the gutter press.

They would be writers!

Life, and rescues, carried on at Lathe Green. The days fragmented by brighter, optimistic light. We savoured these minutes of magic while they were to last. Very early, before the sun was high, you would hear the splashing and flapping of the fitter Swans, warming up and selecting their flight paths. Rina was usually first outside, she would start the feeding and checking at first light. Sheila and I would be in the house, preparing for the day, when the shouting would start. Rina, from a Swan pen.

"One gone!"

"Who this time?" I was struggling into wellington boots and grabbing a camera.

"It's Mrs Ely." Sheila would join us outside.

"Look at her go!"

"And two more."

"It's yesterday's Cygnet."

"Lift little chap, lift!"

"Here she comes again Len, look over the trees!"

"God she's high."

"What a flyer."

"Go on old girl, go on!"

"Look at the speed of that Cygnet."

"Oh look, its poor old Whoopee, he'll never lift, silly old Swan." Sheila now returns to the kitchen to finish making the coffee. I return to check the mail. The splashing and flapping and feeding and checking goes on. A few minutes later, Rina again.

"Here comes Mrs Ely!"

"Rina, coffee's ready."

"Wonder where she's been?"

"We'll never know. Look she's landed!"

"Funny old Swan."

"Cynet's landing, terrible touch down, he'll learn, not enough flaps."

"The other adult has not come back."

"That's good, one away at least."

"Why does Mrs Ely always come back, doesn't she want freedom?"

"Wonder where the other adult will go?"

"Don't know, but, no doubt, we'll see him again."

And we nearly always did. We would collect our friends in black plastic refuse sacks, from beneath the ever present power cable, and drive home without speaking. Each thinking separate thoughts that were to turn out to be identical.

Is it all really worthwhile?

The only thing worse for a Swan, any creature of the wild, or you or I, than dying, is dying twice. Were we guilty of creating more suffering and more dying, by actually rescuing and treating a Swan? In a country already dangerously overcrowded and seemingly hell bent on increasing its population even more, were our actions of altruism also actions of irresponsibility? In our opinion, based unfortunately on bitter experience, there will shortly be no room, in the British Isles, for a creature weighing fifteen kilograms and with a wingspan of some two and a half metres, to fly free. Was there a sky somewhere that was free of power cables, pylons or buildings? Was there a river somewhere that was free of boats and fishermen, where a Swan could simply be a Swan? Were we guilty, through good intent, of releasing Swans into this environment, ensuring further breeding? With total lack of offers of help from individuals, organisations, or Government, who would carry on working for the Swans when we stopped? We all have to die. Life is a terminal disease. Who would take over our mission for the right reason?

Was it morally acceptable to put a Swan through the distress of a rescue chase, dehook or untangle him and put him back into the water for tomorrow's fisherman?

Consider the odds concerning just the fishing. Estimated population of fishermen, four to seven millions (three and a half million licensed). Estimated population of resident British Mute Swans, eighteen and a half thousand. A calculator is not needed to work out the odds. Add to this the power cable situation and it is not surprising that we have to question our own motives in rescuing Swans.

We feel we must mention again another situation that proves disastrous to the waterbird. The barbaric and perverted practice of pinioning Swans and placing them upon lakes and ponds where fishing takes place. This is, unfortunately, quite common practice in Council controlled parks and recreation areas. This can only be compared to us sending our children out to play on a motorway. Pinioning birds is a terrible way to prove that common man has not, and in some cases cannot, come to terms with the fact that he is not the owner of wildlife, but its guardian, or should be. To intentionally injure a bird is, according to the Wildlife and Countryside Act 1983, punishable by a fine. Why then are wildfowl dealers, trusts and the like, apparently outside this law? Could it be that pinioning (cutting off the hand and fingers of a bird) does not, under the pedantic and scientific eyes of the legislator, constitute an injury? The grey area that exists here seems to be the fact that, according to the Act, a captive, sometimes home reared bird is not classified as "wild" and therefore does not come under the "Cruelty to Animals Act", nor any other Act. So, then, no punishable crime of cruelty would seem to exist. If this is indeed the case, according to the law makers, how come it is not only possible, but common for an animal welfare group to successfully prosecute a person for committing an act of cruelty upon his own Dog, Cat, or Horse? When we have questioned the totally incoherent laws pertaining to animal cruelty, the experts tell us that we are studying the wrong law books. The Cruelty to Animal Acts are not used when dealing with a Swan. We needed, they told us, to use the Protection of Birds Act. We did. The Swan is not even listed. When we questioned this we were told by the RSPB that the Swan is indeed covered by the Protection of Birds Act and has the same protection as a wild, common bird. Unlike the Bewick and Whooper Swans, it has no "special" protection. We have never known of a successful prosecution, even an attempted prosecution, to be taken out against a person intentionally cutting off a Swan's hand.

We believe that this act of gross cruelty is tolerated by the higher echelons of animal welfare legal departments because of the embarrassing, to them, fact that certain wildfowl groups are headed by titled people and, sometimes, even patrons, of their societies.

The other "old chestnut" that deserves critical perusal, is the hackneyed phrase, "endangered species". The pinioning of exotic and common birds to ensure trouble free captivity, enabling successful breeding programmes to be carried out. The breeders receive praise from a naive public, for the successful release of such birds to repopulate diminishing, or almost extinct, natural stocks. This is, of course, common practice amongst wildfowlers to add to their shooting stocks. But the people hiding under the, sometimes, dubious banner of "conservation", you would think, would know better. They appear not to.

Surely the question so desperately needing an answer should be: why are this particular species becoming extinct? Is it through, for example, the destruction of their natural habitat? If it is a problem of a diminished environment, where then are you going to release the species you have saved? Is your successful breeding campaign really concerned about the bird, or is it you that needs to feel the sense of satisfaction? There are many grants available, and accolades to enjoy, if you are a successful breeder of exotic birds or animals. You are heading towards the possibility even, of a Knighthood if you release that creature back into its "natural" environment.

If that environment is, for example, the Brazilian Rain Forest, or the hardwood jungles of Asia, then don't you think it is, to say the least, irresponsible to return the bird, Gorilla, or big Cat to a land of desolation?

During the writing of this, we were to watch a BBC TV News item concerning Wood Mice. It seemed to, so graphically, illustrate the above points. Wood Mice were captured from their home within a tiny, threatened, deciduous English forest. Just a few, dying, ancient trees. These delightful, nervous, little mammals, were then taken to a breeding pen and their offspring, if breeding should be successful, were to be released back into their habitat. It would not be a surprise to us if, already, plans are made to build fibreglass and polystyrene oak trees!

What, then, is the answer to abort the declining quality of our country landscape in poor old second-hand Britain?

We do not know. But it may be a good idea to evaluate the seriousness of the problem first, to do this properly and thoroughly. Then take your evidence to the Palace of Yuppydom in Downing Street, and push, push like hell. For you are fighting for a just cause and there can, surely, be no cause as important as the future of this Planet.

As far as animals and birds are concerned there are still, though, moral issues to be evaluated.

It is, to us, of some significance that none of us in the Swan Rescue Service have ever seen, so have never rescued, a suffering Dodo!

CHAPTER 12
Daylight and Dusk

When time allowed we would delight in welcoming the occasional school trip to see our fitter Swans. I enjoy the company of the very young and very old. It is the "in betweens" that I am often uncomfortable with. So the opportunity to welcome, and to show round about a dozen First School children, pleased me. Anyway, at this particular time I had been forbidden by Sheila, Rina and Eddie, to do any physical work. As the time with the Swans went on, I became less able to leap about the rivers and lakes, and the lengthy searches over the marshes were becoming harder and harder as walking became more difficult.

The mini bus arrived at the house and teacher led the small group to where I was standing in a Swan pen. I was to introduce them to Reedham and Ellie, an old pair of breeding Swans. The children crowded around and squealed with delight, as Reedham stood and flapped his magnificent wings. He was a very big Swan. Prompted by their teacher, the children started to ask their usual, very intelligent questions. I was aware of a presence down by my right wellington boot. The presence was Sandra. It was love at first sight. Sandra had blonde hair, tied into plaits, saucer sized blue eyes, no teeth in the front of her mouth and the tiny forefinger of her left hand was thrust up her right nostril. A strange rasping, but squeaky, noise came from Sandra's direction, or seemed to. It sounded like:

"Aseegotafing?"

The teacher had obviously deciphered this strange language, probably hearing it before whilst visiting some strange far distant place or planet. The teacher spoke.

"Sandra!" Is all she said. Teacher then told a little boy to ask a question. Pointing at Reedham the little boy asked.

"How old is he?"

"About five." I answered. Then another little boy, less inhibited now the ice had been broken.

"Do they live long, Swans?"

"They can do, and would if people took care of them." This time a little girl, with a piping bell like voice.

"Why do you call him Reedham?"

"Because we rescued him from Reedham."

"Oh, so if your had rescued him from Norwich, he would be called Norwich, wouldn't he?" She glanced around to the other children, expecting, and receiving their approval.

"Yes I suppose so." I replied. The rasping, squeaking sound again seemed to come from somewhere within the darkness of my right boot.

"Aseegotafing?" It was Sandra. The teacher looked towards her and in a "teacherlike" admonishing tone, said.

"Sandra!" The next question came from a little boy.

"What's that one called over there?" He was pointing at Ellie.

"We call her Ellie." A little girl, hoping to receive the same approval as her friend had previously asked.

"Does she come from Ellie then?" They all burst out laughing, teacher looked at them once. They stopped laughing. It came again, the sound.

"Aseegotafing?"

Sandra!" The teacher's voice now much sharper. The children started giggling, grubby little hands, held palm outwards over their mouths. I looked down at Sandra. Her finger was still thrust up her nostril, her little red boots were planted firmly on the ground, in a pigeon toed position. She was swaying sideways, from her hips. She looked up at me and, smiling, said.

"Aseegotafing?" This time teacher made a light hearted attempt to slap little Sandra's free hand, she didn't actually connect.

"I won't tell you again Sandra!" She said. But Sandra went on.

"Iffeeaintgotafing, thenowduseemakebabies?"

The giggling broke out into howls of uncontrollable laughter.

The rest of the questions were answered and each child, little hands grasping their gifts of Swans feathers and badges, in a Crocodile line, filed back into their mini bus with teacher and disappeared out of our lives.

I only hope that the usually excellent British education system, does much to increase little Sandra's vocabulary and that when, one day, as a beautiful, blonde, blue eyed young lady, when introduced to the young man that could share her life, Sandra does not look up and down and enquire to the person introducing them.

"Aseegotafing?"

The letter we had been dreading finally arrived at Lathe Green. It was confirmed that the farm buildings were indeed going to be sold, and were to be converted into dwellings. The South Norfolk District Council, after their promise, did not tell us. A well wisher had written, feeling it was their duty to inform us of the fact.

We arrived home, one cold day, from a rescue, to find the agent's auction notice firmly planted in the grass frontage of the old farm buildings. We were totally crestfallen. The Council would not do this to us, and the Swans, surely? We had told them that if planning permission was granted for this development, we would probably have to close down the hospital. Now the Council were treating us in the same way, it seemed, as everyone else. They did not even have the decency to either inform us by letter or send someone around to warn us of the impending approval. We unloaded and treated our Swan and, immediately, in an understandably black mood, drove down to the Council offices.

There is a trick practised by Council employees, you are left waiting in a boring reception area for a very long time. This is to make sure that you cool down sufficiently, and so that the hapless clerk has time to compose his speech of apology, They already know who is waiting for them, some magical unseen person will have warned them. We did not need an introduction. He knew who we were. Other people waiting in the reception area coughed nervously and pretended to study the various leaflets, those leaflets that are neatly stacked in little boxes for bored people to use when wanting to write down phone numbers. Employees, seeing the familiar red and white Swan Rescue badges on our jackets, disappeared into those dark, wormlike, corridors that go, presumably, deep into the secret places of Council buildings, where perhaps God dwells, and you never, ever see God. Perhaps the inner sanctum contains the giant computer that gives birth to Civil Servants.

"There is nothing I can do," the young man said, averting our eyes.

"What do you mean nothing?" we protested.

"The plans have been passed," he said.

"But why didn't you let us know?" we queried.

"Oh." His eyes now fixed upon the toe cap of his shoe. "Didn't we?" He fumbled through the file. We were now speaking much louder.

"You know you didn't!"

"We should have done." He continued fumbling through the file and finding a piece of paper, started to read in a weak, very quiet voice.

"Somebody should have written to you."

"Well I can assure you they bloody well didn't, and you know it!" The other people had now moved well away from us and the Civil Servant, some had actually left through the swing doors of the modern reception area. This is a habit of the British – do not get involved. You could have been standing there stark naked, wearing a red clown's nose, and no one, not if they were English, would take the slightest notice. The young Council man had said all that he had rehearsed and now, without a script to follow, seemed to be stuck for words. He stood behind the safety barrier of the counter and tapped the file and its papers on the top, making sure everything was in line, and tidy, Council style. Then, as he walked away towards the womb at the end of the corridor, raised his voice to a slightly higher level and said, over his shoulder, "You can always appeal."

We tried, but when, already labelled as a "crank" or a trouble maker, you try to fight the establishment, you are on a hiding to nothing. The barns would be sold to a developer, we knew that, but when we actually saw the plans that were approved for this development, a mini bijou estate, we hit the roof. The gardens to two of these dolls' house cottages, actually led to, and abutted our hospice pond. The last resting place for our terminally sick Swans. Their final freedom place.

They had won. But what could we do now. After paying the three thousand pounds to the Electricity Board to remove our power cable, more power cables would be needed to supply electricity to the new development. We had spent over £100,000 establishing the finest, most up to date, in fact, the only full time Swan Hospital in the world. All the money from our own pockets, our Swan books and merchandise, we spent on the hospital. The surgery alone, without any fitments, cost over four thousand pounds, another four thousand pounds for water, then sixteen thousand pounds for the filtered swimming pool, and so on, and so on.

But it was obvious to us that we would not be able to carry on at Lathe Green, with four new families, moving directly next to us, and their accompanying cars, dogs and noise. We were totally lost, again.

Were we being told, by some all seeing power, to stop? Were indeed the Swans, in their own age old way of communication without voice, telling us to leave them alone? Were we guilty of being over romantic and far too emotive?

Probably. But the door to emotional escape and romanticism is ever open to the totally disenchanted.

We held a small meeting of all concerned. Sheila, Eddie, Rina and our Swan Lady who had purchased Lathe Green for us. We decided that we had to have a big marsh for our Swans anyway and that this would become the first priority. We had a standing advertisement in the local newspapers for some time but received no replies, so were pessimistic about finding the ideal Swan marsh. Finding a house, however, to convert into a hospital and living accommodation, was a very depressing thought, especially after the back breaking work we had put into Lathe Green. A portion of our lives, no less, had been given to Lathe Green and our Swans, a fragment of our spirit is buried there, with our white friends under the Willow Tree at the back of the garden. Thousands of Swans had been given a second chance at Lathe Green and no one was about to give us a second, or third, chance. For nearly five years there, we had fought, lost, laughed, cried and taken on the entire, it seemed to us, world of doubt and deceit and had in some ways won a lot of battles for the Swan. We would carry on.

Rina and I concentrated again on the estate agents. Sheila would go back into the office, to try and raise some more money sending out Newsletters, and Eddie would continue the rescues alone. Eddie never complained, he never hesitated. If there was a Swan that needed help hundreds of miles away, he was there. But we had noticed that, like us, he too was beginning to feel the strain. For him it had been a period of nearly seven years without a day off.

Never, during mass media campaigns, was Eddie ever acknowledged, never in the limelight, but never wanting to be. He was always working for the Swans and not us. In a country engrossed in materialism, Eddie was out of place, personal gain never entering his mind. His philosophy was always to give, never to take. When at times he arrived back at Lathe Green, with a Swan behind him, and he was soaking wet and very tired after a long journey, his first priority before a hot drink or food, was to help in the surgery. Watching him work on his Swan, acting like a broody Hen, I was moved by remembering that it was Eddie, in those early days of Swan Rescue Service who had, unknown to us, sold his motor bike and sent the money anonymously to the Swans. You can't be anonymous with Swans, they tell you everything! To thank Eddie was to embarrass him. But the Swans thanked Eddie, for they accepted him as their brother.

We carried on with the search, though this was difficult with the telephone ringing from six a.m. to nearly midnight most days. Our Swan Lady had visited us during the search and left an old sale notice, advertising a marsh at Burgh St. Peter, but it was four years old, it would have gone by now. We thanked her and put the piece of paper on the paper mountain in Sheila's office. When passing the mountain, we would occasionally pick up the sale notice, read it, and wonder. Twenty three acres, good land, excellent grazing and a small lake, with long river frontage.

What could we lose? The cost of a phone call. We couldn't resist it. Yes, it was still for sale! We started doing our sums. The land was £29,000, we had, in the Swan Rescue Service charity bank account, £30,000! We had the marsh, or rather the white people did!

We would now try to raise the money for the fencing and set about securing quotations. Ten thousand pound more was needed. We set to work, another Newsletter was rushed out, more books were sold, odds and ends too, and one of our four vans, all transferred into much needed cash. But we had the marsh. There was no stopping us. Our Swan Lady benefactor said we could, if we decided it was best for the Swans, sell the farm and buy a house, if possible near the marsh. So the estate agents were contacted and asked to look out for a suitable place. It did not matter to us what sort of house it was as long as we could convert a part of it to a Swan treatment unit. It would be ideal if it contained a garden, at least, where we could put badly injured Swans to recuperate before releasing onto the marsh.

The supporters again came to the Swans rescue and their generosity was absolutely staggering. They raised just short of the ten thousand pound target for the fencing, we raised the rest.

Eddie and the contractors worked on the fencing. The marsh was ideal, containing many dykes, in excellent condition and with an abundance of aqua vegetation, plus lots of grazing. The river frontage was directly onto the Waveney, the best of the five rivers. Our marsh neighbours were a herd of Friesian heifers owned by a local farmer. No chemical spray had been used on the marsh and it was in beautiful condition, being organic.

We had noticed, on our intitial inspection, that a local dredging company, contracted to the Broads Authority (a toothless consortium set up to manage the Norfolk Broads) had moored their barge to our staithe. We could not have the workmen walking over the marsh and through the Swans, for fear of stress, so asked them if, when time allowed, they could move their barge.

This we believe, started the first murmurs of discontent amongst the xenophobic locals. We had not yet even moved the Swans to the marsh!

During our search for another house the workmen started to prepare the buildings next to Lathe Green for their conversion. Apparently the farmer owner had sold them to a city based company for £150,000. It had become fashionable to live in a barn conversion, they were now featured in the coffee table magazines. The Barn Owl did not approve, if he had, he certainly did not attend the planning council meeting!

The work on the farm building conversions sealed the fate of the Swan Rescue Service hospital. Having a shared right of way with the new neighbours meant that we could not bring in bloody, diseased or moribund Swans in clear view of people overlooking and passing the Surgery. The Surgery door opened onto this shared right of way. With contractors trucks and equipment now blocking our driveway, it was already impossible to carry on.

We are often accused of being bitter. It seemed to us that everybody was out to stop us, and would go to any lengths to achieve their aim. There is no force more powerful than the desire to make money. The farmer who owned the buildings next to our house was a student of Thatcherism, he had graduated with honours.

We continued our search for somewhere to live but, through circumstances totally beyond our control, had been forced to seek a house right in the middle of the housing boom. Prices were, and still are, astronomical.

Whilst the marsh was being prepared for the Swans, we received a telephone call, at Lathe Green, from a very irate farmer. Eddie, for security reasons, had renewed a few strands of old fencing wire over an entrance to our marsh. They had been cut. Thinking this was an act of youthful vandalism, Eddie had simply replaced the wire. The irate farmer told us that we had no right to stop him walking over our marsh. We obviously disagreed. A farmer would have been acceptable if he had good reason, for example checking his cattle, to enter onto our property. But most farmers have dogs, and dogs and captive, disabled Swans do not mix. Apart from this, to allow an open gate onto our marsh, was to encourage the fishermen and shooter onto our land. We tried to explain this to the farmer but he told us that if we blocked his way onto the marsh, he would cut the wire or take down the gate. We warned him not to. So we contacted the Police.

So, it had begun, but we were not going to let one farmer ruin our future with the Swans. We, to safeguard this future, compromised. Eddie would erect a proper gate, we would padlock the gate and give the farmer duplicate keys, to allow him or his stockman, to check his cattle. This we thought was fair and right. What we did not need was confrontation.

At last a house became available. The fact that there was a house for sale so close to the marsh was a miracle. It was exactly a quarter of a mile away. According to the agent it was a large Georgian house in excellent order. Recently renovated to original specification but with the necessary additions, to ensure adequate space for our headquarters. It was detached and set in about one acre. We enquired about the price, and when told looked at each other in disbelief. We were so out of touch with house prices. We received the agents details and put them to one side. When each of us were alone, we secretly studied the coloured photograph and reread the description. We didn't speak much about the house as we knew that we could never raise the money – but it did look perfect, according to the details. One day, when visiting the marsh, we took the opportunity of having a closer look at the house. It was just right.

During her visit to Lathe Green by our Swan Lady, we told her about the house. Without hesitating she offered to borrow money on her house, sell Lathe Green, and buy the house near the marsh.

When the marsh fencing was finished, the Swans were moved out of Lathe Green. They settled straight away into their new home, and devoured the fresh grass, bathed in the small lake, explored the dykes, discovered luscious vegetation and preened and slept contentedly. They were at home.

Eventually Lathe Green was sold and we moved into our new headquarters. We set about converting part of the dairy into an emergency treatment room, built and plumbed in a new Swan bath and wired in the X-ray machine. We used a downstairs room for the dispensary and operating theatre and converted four other rooms to office, store room for books and merchandise and made the largest upstairs room into a studio for Swan publications, shotgun lead and power cable campaign literature and a dark room.

In between her office work and other jobs, Sheila planned and seeded the garden to grow food for us and the Swans. Dear old Luciana, Rina's rescued pet Goat, was given a barn and an old orchard. She was delighted with the gift and devoured the nettles and brambles non stop. She showed her appreciation by running around between meals and kicking her heels to heaven.

So it was that we started upon another journey, down the sometimes dark, but never boring, corridor of life with the Swans.

Our new base was situated in a scattered hamlet, on the borders of Norfolk and Suffolk. The hamlet lacks a centre, a heart. Much like, we were to discover, some of its inhabitants.

We had noticed, when preparing the marsh for the Swans, that we were at times being watched. At least the Swans had noticed, they told us. They would suddenly stop grazing and, necks straight up, would stare out over the marsh, beyond us and to the direction of a gateway. Sure enough, there would be a lone figure of a middle aged man, obviously a man of the soil, simply standing, watching. We have encountered this spectacle many times, whilst living

in East Anglia. He appeared on a few occasions. He resembled from a distance, the farmer who had been born and raised in the house we now occupied. He had moved since, to another farm house, still in this village and not far from us. After meeting him, on moving into our house, we realised they were indeed, one and the same person. The watching continued, he never spoke. We carried on with Swan work and were soon back into the never ending campaigning and rescues.

So now the farmer had keys to our land and their stockman was able to check his cattle and we had presented a polite attitude to our new neighbours. No problems, so we thought. But we were wrong.

The gossip had found its way into the lives of a group of people who were familiar to us, but unknown by us. The "Mafioso" of the English country village. Yes, you've guessed it – the Parish Council. The husband and wife led team of this malevolent core, lived in a little house just up the road from us. We never met them, they delivered their official little letters through our post box under the cover of darkness. The first of their letters told us that they, meaning the people of the village, had used the riverside footpath over our land for years, to walk their dogs and themselves, and that we had no right to block off the entrance to that footpath.

It was not a designated footpath, so we indeed being owners of the land, had every right to ensure its security.

We have always been ambivalent about the rights of ramblers and the like to walk over farmland. We are always interested more in the rights of wildlife than human desires for recreational freedom and all that this entails. Of course we are against restrictions to freedom, whether it be to human or animal. But, as in all things, we have to give and take. If people feel they must walk across land not belonging to them, then they should surely consider what they are doing to the wildlife, before donning their wax cotton jackets and sensible walking shoes. A terrible example of the damage caused by Ramblers was witnessed by Rina and I, whilst on a search rescue for a Swan injured through a power cable collision.

We had noticed that a group of Ramblers had arrived on the same marsh and were walking in the direction of a group of grazing Swans. The Swans, startled by the oncoming Ramblers, took flight, missing the overhead power cables by inches. These people seem to have a God given right to walk anywhere over Britain's countryside. They belong to the same group of intelligentsia as people within organisations of conservation, like for example, the Broads Authority, who restore marshland and riverside wildlife habitats and then create footpaths over and through these areas to allow access by binocular carrying nature lovers. What is the point of creating areas of wilderness and then allowing people entry to that area, thereby destroying that wilderness? This is what the idiot Parish Council were about to do to our Swan Sanctuary.

It happens that right next to our marsh is the power cable mentioned earlier, that took the lives of hundreds of Swans. Ramblers are bad enough but to allow right of way to them also opens up the land to the ever possible chance of vandalism.

We wrote to the Parish Council, the husband and wife, and explained our case to them. They would not listen, however, and had in fact already made application to the County Council in Norwich to have a footpath across our land designated, under a complex law, to be included upon the map as a

Definitive Footpath. If accepted by the County Council, the Godfather of this group of underlinings, then anyone would have the right to walk over our land.

To ascertain the existence of a footpath, it is imperative that you supply the necessary proof, by written statement, that Parishioners have walked that footpath continuously for a period of twenty years. Now this was, of course, no problem for our husband and wife team and their cohorts. They sought out, from their Parishioners, those few who could read and write and talked them into supplying the necessary statements. So the battle began. Yet another unnecessary conflict, we were forced to fight, if we were to carry on our pathetic attempts to help the world's heaviest flying bird. It was enough that nobody ever came to our help over the last eleven years, that our appeals for a better, dignified end of the journey through life of Britain's Swans, had fallen upon deaf ears. But to be attacked throughout this long and difficult journey, shared with our Swans, was, and is, too much to bear.

As an aside, months ago, I had mentioned to our Swan Lady that the only thing that worried me about the new Swan house, was that it was, in its own way, beautiful. She was puzzled by my remark but I explained that one of the most heinous crimes a commoner can commit, in this land of freedom and democracy, especially this area of England, is the attempt to rise above "one's station in life". Although I am extremely proud of my cockney upbringing and comfortable with it, this house was definitely not the house for a group of working class people. It was all right possibly for the chairperson of the local flower arranging society, a hard-up vicar or poor farmer but definitely not for a trio of Londoners, with their dreadful accents and their obviously unhealthy and suspicious attachment to a bird. An aggressive, nasty bird at that.

This may sound like reversed snobbery but I'm afraid it is a fact. We are not, and never have been, welcome in this part of the world. Even when our previous helpers discovered that we had moved into a "nicer" house, the gossip and innuendos started to drift back to us. People who could not face the daily death and destruction of the Swans and had left because of their inadequacies, were now attacking venomously. They were appeasing their own guilt, trying to blacken our name. They had imagined that this house was a magnificent mansion, worth millions of pounds and that we were living in the lap of luxury. None of them, the attackers, however, had ever come to see us or even phoned us, but there are none as blind as those who do not wish to see! A few of these previous helpers had gone their own way, to do their own thing, and now were dissatisfied with that thing, so were hitting us. Our crime being that we had stayed with the Swans. Their problem being that they didn't have the guts to.

Could this all really be happening to us, could people really be this evil? Yes it is and, yes, they could.

All the critics and the doubters, all the traitors and all those with evil tongues and evil minds, could never realise that the only thing that kept us here, in this area, were the Swans. They did not think, or could not understand, that all four of us did have a life before the Swans and desperately wanted to return to it. But unlike them, we stayed and endeavoured to finish the job. If only we could be "normal" again. But we had traded normality for compassion. We threw away all thoughts of self gain and gratification, for a big white bird. How I longed for the peace in the Provence, to feel the warmth, to hear once more the song of the Cicada. To sit under an ancient olive tree or at a pavement cafe, with the distant strains of Jacques Brels music.

Sheila, Eddie and Rina all had other interests and other lives, it is just that we had, according to some, put our priorities into the wrong order. We didn't believe this and we never will.

Rina and I were now spending all our time talking to lawyers, council officials and the like, trying to make some sense out of the chaos caused by local bigots, in this dark and disturbed area of England, and wasting our precious time, trying to understand why we were being so viciously attacked. Faithful Eddie was still looking after the Swans on the marsh. We did not have time now for Swans rescues and decided to terminate our twenty four hour rescue telephone number. We could not take in injured Swans as the "marsh starer" and owner of the land adjacent to our house, had stopped us, in an act of childish belligerence, using the side entrance, a joint right of way to our house. The little, quiet garden area, prepared for incoming Swans, lay vacant. The proposed footpath across our marsh, stopped us putting Swans on their own land. We were being screwed tightly down, they were winning. The mercenaries of conformity are so heavily armed.

Those early questions of morality were once more at the forefront of our minds. Would it really be better, in the long term, for the general public to see suffering and dying Swans, would that daily spectacle shock other people into taking up the challenge and trying to make the environment into a better place for the Swans? After all so many people had told us that they had never seen a suffering or dying Swan. They would now. Had we really done our job too well?

While Rina and I were busy trying to obtain help, the evil ones were talking, planning and speculating. Being a registered charity, our financial accounts, rightly so, were always available to members of the public to scrutinise. This is perfectly acceptable, we had nothing to hide. The fact that nobody ever wanted to know how much of our own money was paid into the charity and indeed at times, actually had kept us going, was irrelevant to the doubters of our credibility. Also of no importance, it seemed, was the fact that none of us, in eleven years, had ever taken a wage from the charity. Always supporting ourselves by our own endeavours.

Now as it was difficult for the public to reach us and while we were suffering what we think now was a complete breakdown, both nervous and physical, it was the turn of the good old British media to turn the knife.

Arriving home one day after a totally fruitless attempt to get sense out of the Norfolk County Council regarding the proposed footpath, Sheila told us she had had a telephone call from Swan Lady. The night before a news item on BBC television had announced that we had disappeared. That more than annoyed us because we were still here. We contacted the producer and he confirmed the fact and, whilst speaking to me, repeated this sensational discovery. I had disappeared, he was speaking to me! Now, you do not need an exceptional amount of intelligence, surely, to realise that the person you are talking to is actually in existence! This was obviously too much for the BBC producer to comprehend. He said, and I quote this exactly:

"If you are there then, perhaps we could interview you." I assured him I was here because I was speaking to him. This seemed to baffle him altogether.

I was now quite ill. Ulcer trouble and total fatigue, brought about by stress, had overtaken me. But I would have to appear on the television to hopefully settle the minds of the people out there who cared about the Swans. I consented to an interview. I have never found it difficult to express my Swan thoughts through the mechanism of the media. I believe in our cause and that gives me all the courage I need.

So it started. Next morning we noticed a car parked out in front of the house. He appeared, Jack the lad, a walking video camera from Anglia television, with the persona of a used car salesman. Before anyone could stop him, his camera was switched on. We stopped the filming and asked him to come into the house. He told us that Anglia TV had sent him and he wanted our story. We asked him why he was filming the house. Already suspecting the man's motives, we asked him to leave. As he left he continued filming the exterior of the house. I told him to stop. I could not understand his need to film the house. I got heavier with him and, asking Rina to phone Eddie for some help, I made sure he stopped filming. Rina then rang Anglia TV to verify whether they had sent a cameraman to our house. They confirmed that they had and, when she explained that the man was pestering us for a story and was filming our house without our permission, he consented to her demand to abort this intrusion of our privacy. They did. But before I had time to give the cameraman this message, he had got into his Sierra and sped away like a formula one driver.

As he left, so the man from the Beeb arrived. He was well known to us, so Eddie relaxed his guard and announced his arrival. I did the interview and it was shown that evening.

We thought the interview was sufficient to dispel the rumours about our disappearance. But this was not the case, instead of satisfying the public by appearing to an audience of thousands and explaining the reasons for not being at their beck and call for

a while, three weeks to be precise, we were pestered further. It is unbelievable that the public accept the fact that most people take at least three weeks' holiday a year and yet we, volunteers all, could not take three weeks' rest in twelve years! It was not exactly a rest, but acute sickness. We were not allowed the privilege of being sick, nor of dying. The public, at large, demanded that we turn out, at any time and on any day, to a sick Swan. After all some individual's out there had sent us a one pound donation some time in the misty past. We were now their property, bought and payed for. What right had I to enjoy peptic ulcers, or suffer a total breakdown? What right had Eddie, Sheila and Rina, to suffer exhaustion and physical ailments?

We had imagined in our naivety, that the BBC interview was enough and that I had explained our position adequately. But this interview was only shown in East Anglia. The trouble makers living locally knew this and wanted, so desperately, to put the boot in. So one particular person, our old friend, the previous helper, contacted one of the Sunday tabloids. He apparently told them that we had left the Swans, were living in a mansion and were not available for twenty four hours a day. The fact that we had recently notified all our supporters of our move, and of our new campaigns for the Swans obviously never reached this evil man. With our address printed in this Newsletter, it would have been pretty difficult to assume we had disappeared!

But this piece of gossip, this childish speculation, was enough for the *Mail on Sunday*. "She" arrived at our house. A child masquerading as an "Environmental Correspondent", together with a camera carrying colleague. She told us that they were interested in the Swans and their story. We, wanting to assure a wide audience that we were still with the Swans, stupidly consented to the interview. When we refused to enter into any discussion regarding money, or matters outside of Swan problems, the child told us that they would print whatever we told them, but if we adopted the "no comment" attitude, they would print a story anyway. She, following the tradition of tabloid journalists, was totally incapable of listening. She never once looked at me, instead asked Rina the questions. I tried to interrupt, but failed. She didn't want the interview to be tarnished by truth. This would never do, she could be sacked for using honesty. She had been sent to dig up filth, and this person had graduated in the school of deceit.

So the story appeared. "Swan SOS Team Faces Cash Probe", it said and went on to say that we were being investigated by the Charity Commission. Rina rang the Charity Commissioners to verify this. They denied the investigation but told her that they had received a complaint, from a person living near to us and had, hoping to appease them made the standard reply. That reply being, to complainees, "We will look into it". This usually satisfied people. There are complaints to the Charity Commissioners all the time and some of them are justified. For example the spending of donations on things other than for that which they were intended. The Charity Commissioners were told by Rina, some three weeks earlier that we were not, at the moment continuing with our actual twenty four hour national rescue service and we were going to try to rest and recuperate to enable us to concentrate on campaign work. This was perfectly acceptable to them and they were a trifle surprised by Rina's insistence that they should be informed. Animal welfare workers were not obliged to warn the Charity Commissioner of impending holidays and were not, obviously, interested in their whereabouts. This has nothing whatever to do with the Charity Trust agreement.

The article in the *Mail on Sunday*, ended by stating that we were living in a Georgian house, paid for by a rich benefactress who was involved with the charity. Our grubby little troublemaker did not know this, however, so it was to prove a great disappointment to him. He had previously spread gossip that I had spent donations on a beautiful house, and was living in luxury. His armour of gross intent now diminished, he must be a very sad, and obviously bitter person. We feel very sorry for him and those other people who have, through their own incompetence, never achieved their dreams or ambitions. It must be a terrible life for them attacking, with pen and paper, those who have dedicated themselves to their chosen cause.

We have not won the battle for the Swans but, nobody, can accuse us of not trying. It is the trying that is important. Our critics have told us many times, how we should have fought and worked for the Swans but none have even tried to do it themselves.

So we were filth. Articles in tabloid newspapers do not have to contain truth. Innuendos are enough, the stigma remains. Letters expressing the fact arrived at our house. Our Swan Lady was pestered by the troublemaker, who wanted the equipment he thought we were now not using, and of course, was after money. So we became prisoners within the old house, not venturing out, being tired of abuse shown by the locals. They do not speak, they stand and stare and occasionally point and snigger. We buried ourselves in our plans for the future and our campaign work for the Swans.

Following an attack upon our Swans at the marsh, by one of the villagers, Eddie moved onto the marsh and stayed on his boat as a permanent security guard with his Dog.

The attack was typical of a person of very little brain. They had used one of our marsh tools to hit out at a nesting Swan. They didn't even have the sense to remove the weapon. It lay upon her nest for some time. Eddie, still thinking of the Swans first and foremost, not wanting to remove it for fear of causing the Swans unnecessary stress.

We will carry on working for the Swans. Our new enterprise is called "SWAN SONG". It is now the time, we believe, to use our pen and our camera,

Attack on our mating pair. Burgh St. Peter Marsh.

rather than our Swan hook and our boats. We believe that after rescuing over seven thousand Swans, we have the experience to enable us to educate and cajole the people of power to start to understand the importance of the welfare of the British Mute Swan, and all the other wildlife, that is suffering, as the result of our needs and greed in a materialistic world. We will never leave the Swans. It is impossible for us to leave them, for they are us, or rather what we would like to be. They are truth, loyalty, hope and freedom. We are not above them, we are not below them, we are with them. When they fly, we fly. When they suffer, we suffer. As long as life sings in us, we will always be in their debt. They have taught us much, but the lessons have only just begun. We are more than willing to carry on that learning.

Until that final day, that very special day, when we, through learning, achieve the wisdom and gentleness that is the Swan.

Photo: Bob Baker.

Len and Loh.

We must always remember . . . after every winter

. . . there will be spring.

Acknowledgements

This book, ten years in the making, was finally brought to fruition, by the generous support of some five hundred Swan lovers. Our special thanks must go to the very young people, that are our inheritors. We hope that they will grow into a better world, made so by their obvious concern for all things of environmental importance. Thank you little people.

My personal thanks to Chief Billy Green (Hopi, New Mexico) and Billy Faithful (N.S.W. Australia) for showing me the way. To Beverley Littlethunder (Sioux, Los Angeles) thanks from Rina, for gently but firmly, pushing her onto a better and more meaningful spiritual path. Our thanks and love to The Onaway Trust, for promoting the message so beautifully.

LEN BAKER

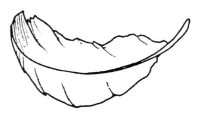